Writing Portfolios

A Bridge from Teaching to Assessment

SANDRA MURPHY

MARY ANN SMITH

Pippin Publishing Limited

Copyright © 1991 by Pippin Publishing Limited
150 Telson Road
Markham, Ontario
L3R 1E5

"Examiner" from *Selected Poems* by F.R. Scott. Used
by permission of the Canadian Publishers,
McClelland & Stewart, Toronto.
"Two Approaches to the Writing Classroom"
reprinted from "Writing: To Assign Is Not to Teach,"
© Cecilia M. Kingston, President, Educational Consultants,
Cecilia Kingston and Associates, Inc., 52 Columbia Ave.,
Hastings on Hudson, New York.

Designed by John Zehethofer
Edited by Dyanne Rivers
Photographs by Kenneth S. Lane
Printed and bound by the Alger Press

Canadian Cataloguing in Publication Data

Murphy, Sandra, 1944-
    Writing portfolios

(The Pippin teacher's library ; 4)
Includes bibliographical references.
ISBN 0-88751-044-2

1. English language — Composition and exercises
— Study and teaching (Secondary). 2. English
language — Composition and exercises — Study
and teaching (Elementary). I. Smith, Mary Ann,
1941-   . II. Title. III. Series.

LB1631.M87 1991   808'.042'0712   C91-094902-6

ISBN 0-88751-044-2

10   9   8   7   6   5   4   3   2   1

CONTENTS

ACKNOWLEDGEMENTS

We wish to thank the following people for making this book possible:

James Gray, Director of the California and National Writing Projects, whose faith in exemplary teachers has permanently changed teaching, learning and the nature of reform in education.

Dale Carlson, Director of the California Assessment Program, who has helped lead California and the nation in the movement towards authentic assessment and, in the process, has taken a risk with us.

Jonathan Lovat Dickson, our editor, whose encouragement and unfailing good humor kept us moving steadily in the proper direction.

Judith Smith, our research assistant, whose conversations with teachers and researchers across the nation, extensive documentations and tireless trips to the library, immersed us in a wide range of portfolio programs and possibilities.

Christine Murphy, our research assistant, whose cataloguing of portfolios and data entry kept the more than 3,000 student writing portfolios in sane, logical and accessible order.

Portfolios teachers at Mt. Diablo High School in Concord, California, and at Jefferson High School in Daly City who deserve to be called "portfolio pioneers," "rugged individualists," and most of all, outstanding teacher scholars.

Portfolio teachers across the country who deserve identical titles and our deep appreciation for sharing what they know and what they do so that other teachers might benefit.

EXAMINER

The routine trickery of the examination
Baffles these hot and discouraged youths.
Driven by they know not what external pressure
They pour their hated self-analysis
Through the nib of confession, onto the accusatory page.

I, who have plotted their immediate downfall,
I am entrusted with the divine categories,
ABCD and the hell of E,
The parade of prize and the backdoor of pass.

In the tight silence
Standing by the green grass window
Watching the fertile earth graduate its sons
With more compassion — not commanding the shape
Of stem and stamen, bringing the trees to pass
By shift of sunlight and increase of rain,
For each seed the whole soil, for the inner life
The environment receptive and contributory —
I shudder at the narrow frames of our text-book schools
In which we plant our so various seedlings.
Each brick-walled barracks
Cut into numbered rooms, black-boarded,
Ties the venturing shoot to the master stick;
The screw-desk rows of lads and girls
Subdued in the shade of an adult —
Their acid subsoil —
Shape the new to the old in the ashen garden.
Shall we open the whole skylight of thought
To these tiptoe minds, bring them our frontier worlds
And the boundless uplands of art for their field of growth?

Or shall we pass them the chosen poems with the footnotes,
Ring the bell on their thoughts, period their play,
Make laws for averages and plans for means,
Print one history book for a whole province, and
Let ninety thousand reach page 10 by Tuesday?

As I gather the inadequate paper evidence, I hear
Across the neat campus lawn
The professional mowers drone, clipping the inch-high green.

F.R. SCOTT (1899-1985)

. . . .

PREFACE

For the past five years, we have been experimenting with portfolio assessment. The "we" in this case are Sandra Murphy, Mary Ann Smith and a large group of California teachers. Twenty of these teachers joined us in a special three-year study, from September 1988 to June 1991, funded by the California Assessment Program, the assessment unit of the Department of Education.

Our research had several important features. First, we were a team. Collaboration meant equal voices, equal authority for making decisions, developing procedures, and collecting and interpreting data. This kind of research led us to collaborate more fully with the students, extending their roles so that they, too, participated in making basic decisions about the design of the portfolio assessment. In other words, we took the usual hierarchical nature of research and turned it inside out.

Second, we made up rules for our research:

— We said, "Volunteers only." That way, our community of researchers could do what professionals should be allowed to do: take the risks necessary to develop exemplary approaches to teaching, learning and assessment.
— We said, "Let's be open to whatever happens." That way, we wouldn't limit ourselves to a single set of questions or hypotheses. We'd avoid the tendency to prove what we'd already predicted. And we'd lessen the

chances of missing something important, something we hadn't anticipated.

— We said, "Okay, we need a working definition of portfolios, something to push off from." We liked the ring of this one: portfolios are a *selection* of student writing for a purpose. We thought it distinguished portfolios from everyday writing folders, which are usually entire collections of writing. It also suggested that portfolios, unlike the typical writing folders, would not sit idle. Someone would have to do something with them.

Third, we allowed ourselves to make mistakes. (We'd have made them anyway, with or without permission.) For example, during the first year we developed some marathon scoring systems for portfolios that left us with enough numbers to start a stock exchange, but not much else in the way of analysis or even satisfaction. We found a scholarly way of describing our mistakes: "This is dumb." And we found ourselves in the classic position of learning from our mistakes as well as our triumphs.

At the same time as we were conducting our research, we — Sandra, Mary Ann and the group of 20 teachers — were working loosely with other California schools in a series of portfolio seminars, again funded by the California Assessment Program. We watched the kinds of decisions the teachers at those schools made in setting up the portfolio programs. They, too, encountered pitfalls, as well as successes. Every assessment program, after all, has its pitfalls. With portfolios, however, we do not have to be stuck in a standardized mold. If the portfolio requirements turn out one year to be too restrictive or not demanding enough, for example, we can alter them the next year. We can do with portfolios what we do with teaching practices: make them more effective over time; continually re-examine, discover and qualify; and continually explore new approaches and theories. In this context, mistakes are not just ordinary mistakes. They are an important part of our lifelong investigations. They get us somewhere.

The 22 of us who conducted the portfolio study are all associated in some way with the Bay Area Writing Project, a university-school collaborative staff development program located at the University of California, Berkeley. The teachers-teaching-teachers model of the project fit right into our way of operating. We served as resources for each other, bringing

8

together our best practices, our own research and our findings from the research of others. This book is, in effect, another teacher-to-teacher effort and a tribute to the rigorous explorations of capable professionals in the schools.

In addition to the work of the California team, this book features the portfolio investigations of teachers across the United States. Our intent is to provide many possibilities, many different ways of deciding about portfolios. Just as there is no single right way of teaching, there is no single right way of going about portfolio assessment. Portfolios invite variation and adaptation.

The book, then, asks two things of the reader:

— A willingness to adapt what's here to your own situation, your own grade level and students.
— An interest in finding out for yourself what portfolios can do for you and the students.

In other words, we hope you will be, as we were, open to whatever happens.

. . . .

WHAT ARE PORTFOLIOS —

AND WHY BOTHER?

A portfolio is more selective than every jot and doodle you do.

Dixie Dellinger

I think teachers need to know that portfolios give kids the responsibility and are not an extra burden on the teacher.

Martha Johnson

Seventeen year old Karen writes at the end of a marking period, "I hate the moment when papers are passed back. I hate getting the dreaded C. I always get Cs."

Her teacher, too, finds little to celebrate in a C grade. She would much rather catch Karen learning than not learning. Catching, however, seems to be the problem. At the moment of truth, when Karen is called on to show off what she knows, she becomes an average student. In fact, she has been an average student for years, the same mark adorning her catch-as-catch-can efforts. She can't seem to rise above it no matter how hard she studies for her tests.

Karen's teacher has reason to be sympathetic. When she was in school, all tests came on Fridays. All reckoning happened on Friday. On that day, students went to school to fill in and match and check. They were steeped in the paraphernalia and ritual of tests: number two pencils, answer keys, bell curves, points, make-ups, posted results. Once in a while, they wrote essay exams. These were shot-gun affairs, timed precisely to the number of minutes in the class period, the topic sprung on the students at the last minute as their pens and pencils hovered over blank paper. Always on Fridays. Always returned with the grammar corrected and the grade in place.

Decades later, many students are still drumming up "right" answers and writing essays to the tick of a clock. They're still the mere recipients of topics and tests. They still respond almost mechanically, taking in facts and echoing them back, unless, like Karen, their automatic gear malfunctions. In short, they are too often reproducers of knowledge rather than producers.

Consider a second, even more discouraging situation. For years, students like Karen have also taken standardized or commercial tests — for the purpose of getting in or out of school, or for proving mastery or achievement. These external tests, often served up as multiple choice questions, are, by design, divorced from the classroom and school curriculum. Teachers and students have two options. They can ignore the tests altogether, treating them as foreign objects that will mysteriously measure "pure" learning. Or they can sacrifice the curriculum to prepare for the tests. Often this preparation calls for attending to small, unrelated skills or for practicing lightning-speed responses to surprise writing topics. Either way, the messages passed on to students are damaging:

— What happens in the classroom is not as important as what happens during the test.
— Doing well on tests is the result of something other than diligence, determination and effort.
— Students have no role, authority or voice in showing what they have learned.

This book is about a third kind of assessment. The main participants are students and their teachers. Together, they share all responsibility for assessment. Let's look at another student and his teacher to see what might happen when this kind of assessment takes place.

Ronald Cabiltes is 14 years old. When he comes to his first-year English class in September, the teacher, Mr. Martin, hands him two folders. "The first folder," the teacher says, "is your writing folder. I want you to put all your writing in this folder, every draft."

"This is your portfolio," his teacher says about the second folder. "Every so often you'll choose a piece from your writing folder and put it in your portfolio. I'll ask you to write about why you picked that particular paper and what you intended when you wrote it. I may also ask you to write about how you wrote it, what special problems it posed for you and what it taught you about writing. Later in the year, you'll submit your

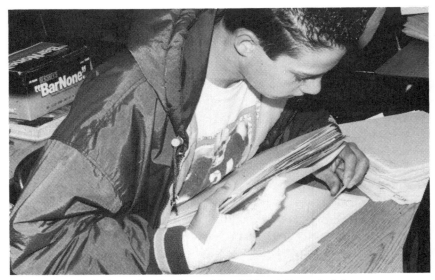
A ninth grader files his writing folder at the end of class.

portfolio to the English department. You'll write a letter of introduction to your portfolio, justifying each choice and talking about yourself as a writer — your strengths and weaknesses. In other words, you'll have the main responsibility for preparing and presenting your work for evaluation. You may revise your writing all you want to get it ready. I'll be working with you on the writing and on the specific things the teachers will be looking for when they read your portfolio.

"Next year your portfolio will follow you to your sophomore class and, once again, you'll fill it with the writings you choose as most representative of your work. By June of your senior year, you'll have more than a diploma or a string of grades. You'll have a portfolio filled with the work you did while you were here, a record of what you learned. You'll be an author, leaving school with a collection of your most important writings."

Then Mr. Martin tells Ron and his classmates that all the English teachers will benefit from the portfolios too:

— They'll be able to see which lessons work well.
— They'll examine the curriculum by looking at real papers, collected over a period of time.
— They'll talk about what kind of writers they want their students to be and then look at what kind of writers they're becoming.

— They'll concentrate on growth and development instead of a one-time performance.
— They'll see how students manage the writing process.
— They'll learn how students perform different kinds of writing.

We'll return to Ron in each of the chapters that follow. For the moment it's important to note that Ron's introduction to portfolios is only one of countless possibilities. There is no single right way to approach portfolios. One intent of this book is to present a range of portfolio practices.

For the purposes of this book, we will also make three assumptions. The first is that evaluation and assessment are the same thing. We'll use the terms interchangeably. The second is that portfolios, as distinguished from writing folders or other collections of writing, contain selections made for a purpose. Our final assumption is that teachers should not go blindly into the messy business of portfolio assessment without looking at how this evaluation method differs from traditional testing.

The Problem with Traditional Testing

Common sense tells us that any attempt to judge student writers based on a single writing sample collected on a single occasion is bound to be inadequate. A student's success with one kind of writing, after all, does not ensure success with another. Further, it is impossible to take a student's performance on a single occasion and use it to predict what will happen on others. In fact, uniformity of any kind is impossible. No matter how precise the set of directions for a particular writing task, it's likely that at least one student will venture beyond the parameters of the assignment. (If it weren't for students, evaluation would be so much more efficient!)

Traditional testing cannot accommodate the student who is too creative or who has an alternative reading of the task. With traditional tests, there is a standard, a "right answer" if you will, that is non-negotiable and used as a basis for sorting students into categories. In other words, students are treated like peas and beans, the category they fall into decided by how closely their performances match the predetermined "ideal."

The pea-and-bean approach to testing leaves no room for the "in-betweens."

The chart on the next page outlines the differences between traditional assessment — the pea-and-bean approach — and alternative approaches that exemplary classroom practice and research tell us we need.

Charts are, of course, deceptively neat. Alternative approaches like portfolios are not so neat. They demand tolerance of bulky folders full of writings and works-in-progress. In addition, portfolios — or, indeed, any innovations in education — never provide THE ANSWER. Portfolios can, however, make this claim: they can make sense of the day-to-day fray by telling what students have learned, how they've learned, and what has helped them learn.

Decisions about Portfolios

On the one hand, portfolios are a set of artifacts. On the other, they represent a set of decisions. The benefits of portfolios lie as much in the decision-making processes they initiate as in the range of products they contain. Suppose, for example, that two neighboring teachers sit down together to talk about why they might experiment with portfolios. Each tells the other what's important about collecting student writing. They unveil their philosophies, their hopes and, perhaps, their doubts. They talk about the look of portfolios, what might be slipped between the flaps. Soon they're talking about their teaching and how it's likely to proceed if portfolios are introduced. In other words, the conversation about portfolios evolves to encompass the subjects of classroom practice and theory. Both teachers will also talk to students and that talk, too, will lead to new insights into teaching, curriculum and learning.

If schools are to have a "thinking curriculum," to borrow a term used by Lauren and David Resnick in a proposal they wrote for the Learning Research and Development Center, the thinking about the curriculum itself, about what's worth doing and knowing, must come from teachers and students. Portfolios are one vehicle for encouraging this kind of thinking. We urge teachers and students to take full advantage of this opportunity to make decisions, letting each become an exploration of the way things are and could be.

PEA-AND-BEAN APPROACH	ALTERNATIVE APPROACHES
A command performance: students are asked to write on demand in a given length of time.	Student writers have time to weave their way to final copy, by recursive processes of writing and revising.
Processes, if considered at all, are regimented (e.g., by time and/or by prescription of the prewriting exercise).	Processes are regarded as individual and dynamic; that is, the individual may use different processes in different writing situations.
Students are asked to show what they have learned.	Students are asked to use writing as a tool for learning.
Students are often compared to other students.	Students are compared to themselves.
Students are the subjects of tests.	Students are responsible for showing what they've learned.
Someone else evaluates students.	Students are also responsible for evaluating their own learning.
Students, regardless of how much they've progressed, are measured the same way year after year.	Students, in recognition of their progress, can be assessed in different ways each year.
Students are usually not allowed to talk or ask for help.	Students are encouraged to use their teachers and classmates as resources.
Students and their teachers receive minimal information from tests.	Students and teachers generate complex information about teaching and learning from assessment.
Tests typically measure one-time performances.	Tests examine growth and development.
Tests commonly provide limited pictures of individual performance (e.g., one or two types of writing).	Tests provide multiple snapshots of students writing for different purposes and audiences.
Tests mark endpoints.	Tests mark beginnings.
Tests may operate independently.	Tests are anchored in learning and curriculum.

To this end, we have organized this book around key decisions in portfolio assessment. Each chapter deals with a particular question and describes how various teachers have addressed it. We emphasize the importance of considering each of the following decisions with a certain classroom, school or group of students in mind:

— What are the purposes of portfolio assessment?
— Who is the audience for the portfolios?
— What goes into the portfolios?
— Who selects what goes into the portfolios?
— How much goes into the portfolio?
— What happens to the portfolios?
— Who hears about the results?
— What are ways to communicate results?
— What are possibilities for revising the portfolio program?

. . . .

WHAT ARE THE PURPOSES

OF PORTFOLIO ASSESSMENT?

Portfolios are for the kids to look at their own growth.

Linda Rief

The students fret and stew. They claim that none of their pieces go together. They have to go through trials and tribulations to decide what fits.

Dan Kirby

Let's return for a moment to the case of Ron Cabiltes. When his English teachers met to talk about the forthcoming portfolio project, they began by listing all the possible purposes for using portfolios. The conversation began something like this:

"Why do we want to do this?"

Silence.

"How about to make our students feel like writers?"

"Okay, to motivate them."

"You mean to motivate us."

"Yeah. To look at what we're teaching."

"And how we teach."

Silence.

"I want to see if the kids' writing has improved."

"They should care about their writing, be responsible."

One teacher recorded all the proposed purposes on the chalkboard. The idea was to wring out every possibility, no matter how remote, and, afterwards, to consider carefully which purpose or purposes made sense in terms of their school, its students and teachers. Among the possible purposes, they suggested using portfolios to:

— Document student growth over time.

— Motivate and empower students, encouraging a sense of ownership and accomplishment.
— Establish or examine the teaching of writing as a process.
— Provide a focus for discussing teaching strategies with other teachers.
— Review student performance periodically.
— Provide a focus for conferring with students about their writing.
— Help students learn how to evaluate their own writing.
— Look at how students write in particular modes.
— Establish or examine a school-wide writing program.

After all the teachers had their say, they saw that the purposes listed fell into two broad categories: student purposes (e.g., empowering and motivating students as writers and encouraging self-assessment) and teacher purposes (e.g., examining teaching strategies and assessing performance). Any decent method of assessment, they decided, should serve both teachers and learners. Therefore, theirs would include purposes for both.

Why Is Purpose Important?

When they teach, teachers think about why they give a certain assignment or guide the class in a particular direction. When they assess students, they also want a clear sense of what it is they're trying to accomplish. The first consideration, then, in any portfolio program, is its purpose. In fact, the decision about purpose affects all the other decisions teachers make about portfolios.

Imagine an artist selecting pieces for a portfolio with no sense of what the portfolio is to represent. For what — or whom — is it intended? However, if there is a reason for creating the portfolio — say, to apply for a job or to persuade a gallery to arrange an exhibit — then the artist has a basis for making selections: to demonstrate range and versatility, perhaps, or to contribute watercolors for a show on watercolors. The same is true of writing portfolios. They need a reason to be. Here are some other purposes for portfolios, gathered from various portfolio programs across the country:

— Help parents understand their child's efforts and progress.
— Promote and examine writing across the curriculum.
— Allow students to earn credit in first-year college composition.
— Allow students to document skills and knowledge acquired through life experiences (e.g., volunteer activities, military or corporate training, independent reading, etc.).
— Help students prepare for a job search.
— Provide an authentic way of communicating to students, parents and other teachers the specifics of a student's performance.
— Encourage students to revise and systematically analyze their revision strategies.
— Provide students with the opportunity to analyze and assess their own growth and thinking tracks.
— Provide students with an avenue for reflection and for setting personal goals.
— Inform and reform curriculum.
— Provide a basis for making teaching decisions and setting teaching goals.
— Examine the nature of different writing tasks and/or distinguish the writing situations (purpose, audience and content area) in which students are most successful.
— Develop insights into second language learning and into the activities most effective for bilingual learners.
— Provide for better staff communication.
— Provide information for the next year's teacher(s).
— Identify school strengths and areas needing improvement.
— Provide program evaluation.
— Provide staff development for teachers.
— Replace other kinds of tests.
— Serve as a vehicle for student publication.
— Provide a basis for discussion among teachers at different grade levels and schools.
— Determine placement and, in particular, open up honors and advanced placement classes to students whose standardized test scores prevent their participation.
— Decide on common ingredients, standards or criteria that apply to all students' work.

— Serve as a vehicle for changing the school's conversations with the public.

This list, of course, does not begin to approximate the range of possible purposes for using portfolios. It does, however, suggest that purposes may vary widely and, therefore, portfolio programs can go in a variety of directions. A portfolio program that emphasizes writing to learn, for example, might look quite different from one that exists to document how students have met their personal writing goals.

How Do Purposes Affect Classrooms?

Many teachers use portfolios to reduce the paper load. Rather than responding to individual exercises and papers, they read only those papers that students have selected as most representative of their best work. This purpose affects not only the contents of the portfolio, but the fabric of the class itself. Behind this schema for portfolios lies a belief that student writers should be able to practice writing frequently without having every attempt graded. Too, teachers should be able to teach writing without having to touch or assess every paper.

Some portfolio classes take on the characteristics of an art studio. This is especially true of classes in Pittsburgh's Arts PROPEL (PRO for production, R for reflection, PE for perception and L for learning) Project, a cooperative research project involving the Pittsburgh public schools and Project Zero, an arts education research effort in the Harvard Graduate School of Education. The purpose is to use portfolios for reflection and artistic learning in visual arts, music and imaginative writing. Teachers in PROPEL classes ask students, as Dennie Palmer Wolf says, "to read their own progress in the 'footprints of their work,'" to "return to their collections of work, taking up the stance of an informed critic or autobiographer, noticing what is characteristic, what has changed with time, or what still remains to be done." Like artists, students keep both working and final portfolios. Students revisit working portfolios periodically, to see whether "old favorites hold up in the light of their own evolving standards," to assess their own development as writers and to find pieces that can be picked up and continued or taken in new directions. They cre-

Ninth graders work together to revise their papers.

ate final portfolios at the midpoint or end of the year and these are passed along to the next set of teachers.

In PROPEL classrooms, and in others with an art studio approach, students create extended projects. Dan Kirby, for example, invites students to write several related pieces such as a series of explorations of early childhood. Then he asks them to link three of those pieces into a unified whole, a process he calls "scheming the piece." In Kirby's class, the classroom-as-studio metaphor extends to display as well. Students place portfolios containing their best pieces of writing in a gallery, a special space on the classroom wall. Students from other classes drop in to look at the portfolios. These students write comments to the authors on stick-it notes and place them on the portfolios. The purpose in this case is to use portfolios as a vehicle for appreciating students' accomplishments.

These examples illustrate that the success of portfolios, in meeting their particular purposes, depends on the classroom climate. The Arts PROPEL Project would not thrive in a setting that did not include ample opportunities for writing, reflecting and revising. Kirby's students would have little to display in the gallery if they wrote little. The examples go on and on. If the purpose of portfolios is to look at how well students write in different modes or for different audiences and purposes, then students need diverse writing experiences. If the purpose is to examine how students manage writing processes, then students need instruction in processes. In short, classroom practices and portfolio assessment go hand in hand.

What Classroom Practices Are Essential to Any Purpose?

Without doubt, writing portfolios have a better chance of succeeding when the teacher actively teaches writing. The chart on the following pages, prepared by former English teacher Cecelia Kingston, who is now an education consultant, dramatizes the importance of active teaching.

To this chart, now add the notion that students, too, must be active learners if portfolios are to succeed. They benefit from these classroom conditions because they are provided with:

— Time to engage in reading, writing, speaking and listening.
— Permission to make choices about what to do, how to do it and what to do next.
— Permission to take risks, make mistakes, attempt new things.
— Opportunities for daily interaction with adults and peers.
— Support and practice in observing, rediscovering and reflecting on their own work and the work of others.

Deciding on Purposes: Issues and Concerns

HOW MANY PURPOSES?

While the possible purposes for a portfolio program are unlimited, it makes sense to set practical limits. Just as a single classroom lesson cannot teach everything, a single portfolio assessment cannot evaluate everything. Thankfully. Teachers have permission to start small, to choose two or three purposes — a manageable number that also provides a clear focus for the assessment.

When Writing Is Assigned	*When Writing Is Taught*
Teacher asks students to select topic from a list that may not be related to course content or students' experiences.	Teacher encourages students to communicate their ideas precisely in writing.
Topic or question is usually general, rarely structured.	Topic or question is usually specific, often highly structured.
Topic allows for sloppy thinking, glittering generalities.	Topic forces precise thought, supporting details.
Audience for paper is rarely identified.	Audience for paper is specifically identified.
Purpose for writing assignment is nebulous or vague.	Purpose for writing assignment is specifically stated.
Students assume they are writing for a grade.	Students know they're writing to improve ability to express themselves precisely.
Students are often asked to write spontaneously.	Students are encouraged to think about their subjects.
Students are often given a time limit or work limit or both.	Students are encouraged to judge the scope of the purpose in terms of time available and number of words necessary to fulfill purpose.
Students are required to hand in the first draft for a grade.	Students are encouraged to review and revise the first draft.
Teacher comments on paper are usually negative, most often corrections of errors.	Teacher comments stress the positive and are constructive about the negative aspects.
Corrections usually refer to mechanical errors.	Recommendations for improvements in style, format and organization are made.
Teacher usually corrects every error on every page.	Often only certain elements of composition — errors — are corrected for a specific assignment.

Most of the teacher's time is spent correcting papers.	Most of the teacher's time is spent in class teaching the writing skills.
The teacher corrects every paper.	The teacher encourages self-evaluation and group evaluation of most of the papers.
Students never quite know how grades are arrived at.	Students always know why they earn a grade.
All writing assignments tend to be essays — usually between 200-300 words.	Writing assignments vary in length according to the purpose of the assignment.
Students are criticized for not making purpose clear, not organizing thoughts logically or not developing ideas.	Students are taught how to limit purpose, organize thoughts and develop ideas.
Students are not aware of significant improvements in their writing.	Students are aware of significant growth — or lack of it — in specific areas.
Students are asked to analyze, compare, describe, review, trace, but are not taught how to organize their thoughts to succeed in achieving their goals.	Students are given models of essays that analyze or compare, etc., and/or they are guided into developing the format best suited for analysis or comparison, etc.
Students are required to rewrite — sometimes. This usually involves only correcting grammar, usage, etc.	Students are encouraged to revise, to edit, to improve — and to correct first draft, then resubmit.
Students are required to write without much *prethought*.	Students are motivated to think about what they are to write.
Students rarely know what style means or what their own style is.	Students are taught to analyze their own style.
Students are assigned a number of different writing experiences: poem, play, book review, term paper.	Students are taught to handle a variety of writing forms.
Students and teacher are bored by students' writing.	Students and teacher are excited about students' writing.

Purposes need not be cast in stone. In classroom situations, a change in purpose can help learning. On one occasion, for example, a teacher might ask students to select papers that show how well they can adjust their writing to different audiences. On another, they might be asked to choose papers that demonstrate clear organization or use of specifics to support a point. Here, the purposes change with instructional goals and, in the process, reinforce notions such as writing for a particular audience.

The same flexibility can apply to department or school-wide portfolio programs. Teachers can renegotiate purposes from year to year in light of what they and their students learned from their previous efforts. In contrast to assessments that have a single purpose for all time, portfolio programs can reflect the dynamic nature of teaching, learning and curriculum.

CAN ALL KINDS OF PURPOSES COEXIST?

Regrettably, purposes have a nasty habit of becoming contradictory. Let's say teachers want to look at how students write in defined situations or in response to particular assignments. At the same time, they want to use the portfolios to heighten the students' sense of themselves as authors. The contradiction hinges on who selects the papers for the portfolios: the teacher or the student? Teacher selections are more likely to guarantee that the designated pieces will show up in the portfolio. On the other hand, student selections, which promote feelings of authorship, can be personal, occasionally whimsical, choices, possibly far removed from the teacher's wishes. Purposes that accommodate each other keep the portfolio program from becoming muddy and frustrating.

. . . .

WHAT GOES

INTO PORTFOLIOS?

When students choose the contents of the portfolios, they are more motivated to revise and change.

Will Lindwall

For years, afterwards, anybody can go back and see what the students were taught and how they were taught.

Don Cecil

Our 14-year-old Ronald Cabiltes made these selections for his ninth-grade portfolio:

— A childhood memory about (what else?) his first home run.
— An opinion paper about soccer.
— An entry from his journal about a bad luck day.
— A descriptive piece about pain.
— An open letter to Colonel Sanders: topic — chicken vs. submarine sandwiches.
— A speculation: "If I were stranded on a desert island."
— A letter introducing his portfolio, addressed to his teacher and signed, with the bravado of a young man, "Your best student."

These pieces were not selected at random. Ron's teacher and his colleagues arrived at a framework for the contents by telling each other what they taught behind the closed doors of their classrooms. They found commonalities — "Oh, you do journals too?" — and a willingness to agree on certain writing situations that seemed right for all the ninth-grade students. By writing situations, they meant the broad categories reflected in the preceding list rather than specific assignments.

When Ron turned 15 and became a sophomore, his teachers experimented with a different framework for selecting contents. Instead of specifying types of writing — letter, opinion, speculation — they specified writing strategies. Their instructions to the students sounded something like this: "Select a piece for your portfolio that shows you know how to state and support an opinion (how to revise, how to use writing to reflect, etc.)." In other words, the students were invited to select from many different types of writing as long as they demonstrated the strategy in question. Again, the teachers' choice of strategies to assess emerged from discussions of what they taught and what they deemed important to teach.

How Does Purpose Affect Portfolio Contents?

Purpose, in fact, governs what will go into the portfolio. Let's consider a planned portfolio program in the state of Vermont, where contents reflect a set of complex purposes. The Vermont teachers intend to use the portfolios to evaluate school writing programs. Embedded in that purpose are several assumptions or expectations about what good writing programs are like:

— They offer students diverse writing experiences.
— They encourage and support writing in all disciplines.
— They view writing as a process.
— They value student reflection.
— They focus on individual growth and development.

The contents of the Vermont portfolios, then, are directly tied to these assumptions:

— The contents include a range of writing in order to demonstrate the variety of assignments and lessons students encounter in a writing program, from poems to personal narratives, from writing about reading to writing about events.
— The selection criteria call for "prose pieces from any curriculum area that is not English or language arts," thereby stimulating or recognizing the importance of writing in other disciplines.
— The criteria require that students include their "best piece" and describe how they wrote it. In other words, students in this portfolio program are asked to make explicit the processes they use to write.

— The selection process promotes reflection by the students. They explain in reflective letters their choice of a best piece.
— The contents are dated so that individual progress can be charted over time.

It's worth noting that the selection criteria for the Vermont portfolios confine neither teachers nor students to a specific (or external) curriculum. The emphasis is on program characteristics.

What Are Some Options for Selecting Portfolio Contents?

What follows are some suggestions for selecting the contents of writing portfolios, each possibility tied to a specific purpose. Note that, in every case, the suggestions include opportunities for students to reflect on their writing.

If the purpose is to promote and examine writing across the curriculum, portfolio contents might include:

— A "best" or "most representative" piece from each discipline.
— A piece in which "you learned something you didn't know before."
— Different kinds of writing (e.g., oral histories, journals and diaries, autobiographical sketches, historical fiction, stories, lab reports or letters, scripts, etc.).
— Extended projects (e.g., newspapers, magazines, children's books, I-Search and research projects, pieces around a theme).
— Written reflection on writing to learn and on writing in different disciplines.

If the purpose is to examine the teaching and learning of writing as a process, portfolio contents might include:

— Process entries — all prewriting for, drafts of and responses to each finished piece.
— A written reflection on the process involved in writing each piece or collection of pieces and on the routines that help the student writer.
— Work(s)-in-progress, with the author's written plans for revision.

If the purpose is to examine growth over time, contents might include:

— Several samples collected at regular intervals (e.g., personal experience papers collected each quarter).
— Initial products with revisions made later in the year.
— Dated papers organized chronologically according to a particular principle or strategy (e.g., papers that demonstrate organization, use of detail, sentence variety, focus, persuasive evidence).
— A written reflection on the student's progress.
— Student-constructed rankings of papers from least to most effective with commentary.

If the purpose is to focus students' attention on in-depth explorations and areas of concentration, contents might include:

— A series of pieces around a theme, a genre, a particular purpose or audience.
— Documentation of the evolution of an extended project (e.g., selected sketches and interviews for a biography).
— A written reflection on the organizing principle, the process and the products.

If the purpose is to help students prepare for a job search, contents might include:

— An application letter and resume.
— An autobiographical piece or self-introduction.
— Samples representing the range of the students' experiences and abilities with commentary.

How Can Portfolios Include a Wide Variety of Writing?

Another way to shape the guidelines for selecting portfolio contents is to consider the form, purpose and audience for the writing. When a purpose is to look at student achievement or development across a range of writing, these classifications might be helpful:

— What ? This refers to the genre or form (e.g., story, script, letter, narrative, poem, biography, autobiography, editorial, review, report, journal, diary).

— Why? This refers to the purpose (e.g., to inform, evaluate, interpret, entertain, persuade, argue, reflect, solve problems, speculate).

— To Whom? This deals with the audience (e.g., self, peers, younger child, trusted adult, unfamiliar individual, general audience, employer, family member, principal, editor, celebrity, teacher as examiner).

How Can Portfolios Show Writing Processes?

In the Arts PROPEL Project, portfolios are actually called "process-folios." Students include both finished works and biographies of works explaining the stages in the development of a piece. These biographies may include journal entries students have made along the way to reflect on the processes of writing. They may also include all the notes and drafts telling the story of a piece. In this way, portfolios become long-term records that allow teachers and students to examine how processes change and how students learn to manage them more effectively.

What Should Students Know about Assembling Contents?

Mt. Diablo's Jan Bergamini wants her students to revise once more as they assemble their portfolios. To this end, she gives them the following checklist for each piece they will include. The checklist directs them to collaborate with others when making their revisions. This takes no control away from students. Rather, it reminds them of what students do when they are in control of the revision process:

PORTFOLIO PROJECT

Revision   — To look back and change for the better
            — To "re-vision"
            — To improve upon

CHECKLIST

As you revise papers for your portfolio, use this sample checklist to help you.

1. I talked to _____ about this piece of writing.   _____

2. I revised this piece of writing as follows:
   Length — I expanded my ideas, wrote more.   _____
   Content — I provided more support, examples.   _____
   Editing — I removed repetition, made sentences
   more concise, tightened my paragraphs.   _____
   Mechanics — I corrected for:
   Spelling.   _____
   Grammar.   _____
   Punctuation.   _____

Teachers at San Diego High School are explicit with their students in order to guide portfolio choices. As students assemble their interdisciplinary portfolios, they can refer to the actual evaluation criteria. In social studies, for example, students can take into account guidelines such as:

— Uses historical evidence to support arguments and ideas.
— Uses creativity to approach and convey ideas.
— Expresses ideas clearly.
— Connects historical periods with today.
— Demonstrates an understanding of cause-and-effect relationships.

In mathematics, on the other hand, the guidelines are different and may include:

— Demonstrates the problem-solving process.
— Uses logical reasoning skills.
— Draws conclusions by deductive reasoning.
— Shows revision.
— Uses creativity to approach and convey ideas.

Students can only benefit from knowing, rather than guessing at, expectations. Many teachers collaborate with students in making decisions about contents and other aspects of the portfolio program. This way, students can understand the guidelines from the inside out.

At Oyster River Middle School, Linda Rief has developed a system that puts the authority for assembling portfolios in the hands of the students. After several weeks of intensive writing, students select two pieces to revise for their portfolios. At the end of 12 weeks, the portfolios contain four revised pieces. The students then arrange the pieces in order of effectiveness

— from the most effective to the least. In small groups and then with Rief's help, students develop criteria by which to order and analyze their papers. As the contents of the portfolio build with each writing, selecting and revising cycle, the order of the contents changes. In this way, Rief takes full advantage of the assembly process to teach students more and more about writing, revising and self-evaluating.

Can Students Include Out-of-Class Writing in Portfolios?

At Miami University in Ohio, students may write papers for their portfolios in class or out of school. They may also revise papers at any time. Because the portfolios provide an alternative route to fulfilling the university writing requirement, these conditions mirror the way student writers write in first-year English classes at Miami. Contrast these conditions with the traditional criteria for exempting students or placing them in advanced classes: timed writings (sometimes one after the other), surprise topics, silence. Real writers — at Miami or elsewhere — do not thrive in these circumstances. The thinking at Miami, then, seems to be that students deserve the best shot at producing their best work — the same shot, in fact, they would have in the class they are seeking to sidestep.

A similar philosophy prevails at Mt. Vernon High School in Fairfax, Virginia. All students are invited to submit portfolios to apply for a seat in the advanced placement gifted and talented class (APGT). Teacher Bob Ingalls gives the applicants carte blanche, free rein to prepare the best possible portfolios. As a result, more minority students are taking advanced classes today. Previously barred by their standardized test scores, these students, according to Ingalls, now have "an option that lets them shine." Ingalls also notes that students who entered the APGT class without a portfolio, in other words by virtue of a single test score, work less hard in the class than those who came with portfolios.

Deciding on Contents: Issues and Concerns

HOW MANY PIECES CAN A PORTFOLIO CONTAIN?

While portfolios are infinitely expandable, there is good reason to limit the number of entries. Quite simply, titanic portfolios are "hellacious" to read, John Winbury of Black Mountain Middle School reminds us. Portfolios are, after all, a selection rather than an entire collection. They are intended to be representative — a sampling of what students can do. They are also intended for an audience. We cannot expect any audience — not even a prospective employer — to examine a huge folder. At the same time, one or two pieces does not a portfolio make. Portfolio readers need enough material to develop a picture of a student's performance and make judgments or generalizations about a writer-in-progress.

WHO SELECTS THE CONTENTS OF THE PORTFOLIO?

Someone must decide what goes into portfolios. The most likely candidates for this task are, of course, the student or the teacher, or both. There are good arguments for letting students make the choices. In his article, "Self-Assessment and the Mastery of Writing," E.H. Thompson comments, "In our rush to test students these days, we frequently forget that assessment should provide information for students, as well as for teachers and administrators. According to Lev Vygotsky, only when students are able to detach themselves from the creative task at hand and view their efforts objectively are they in a position to achieve mastery over any cognitive task they are engaged in. This is especially true of writing. After all, when students write something, someone has to make a judgment about its effectiveness. Why not let this 'someone' increasingly become the student?"

Student choice, then, fosters learning and achievement in writing. Listen to this eighth grader as she introduces her self-selected portfolio pieces to her teachers at a California urban middle school:

Dear Readers,

I don't consider myself a good writer. I think my writing technique is juvenile. My stories are mostly imaginary; I write about things that couldn't possibly happen in real life.

I like writing poems a lot. I guess you can say that I have a thing for words that rhyme. I think my poems are some of my best writings. I prefer to write poems overall because they can make sense without actually making sense.

When I write, or prepare to write, I first think about what I'm about to write for about 10 minutes, then I brainstorm on paper, then I make a rough draft, then a final project. I have learned to reread and how to edit my own papers and others' papers since I have been at this school. I have also learned how to write papers showing description and not telling; this has been emphasized during my three years at this school.

My best piece of writing is my story entitled, "Beware of Me." I feel this is my best writing because it is very descriptive and informative. I enjoyed writing this piece because I got to choose my own topic. The story was very fun to write and it let my imagination sour. (Perhaps she means "soar.")

If I had to evaluate my own portfolio, I would give myself an "A" because it has all of my own thoughts and it's my piece of work.

Sincerely,
Yolanda Washington

Note that Yolanda has a change of heart from the beginning of this letter, when she labels herself "juvenile," to the end when she awards herself a top mark. Because Yolanda selected the pieces for her own portfolio, she had to evaluate her writing. She also had the opportunity to evaluate her writing processes. Picture Yolanda grimly leafing through her writing folder for what she wants to put in the portfolio. She's prepared for the worst but what she discovers isn't so bad after all. The writing she chooses is descriptive, "show don't tell," and if she's allowed to choose her own topic or write a poem, she's in good shape. If someone else had made the choices for Yolanda, she might never have had these particular insights.

Beyond the learning that happens for Yolanda and her classmates when they make their portfolio selections, simple logic and fairness dictate that those who are being examined should have some responsibility and authority for choosing what products — and processes — are suitable and fit for examination. Further, by exercising this kind of personal judgment, students are practicing a life skill; that is, emulating the kinds of decisions adult workers must make.

Teachers may wish they could choose some of the portfolio entries as well. There are certainly no rules restricting a teacher's role in the selection process. Rather, the issue is ownership. Does the portfolio belong to the student or to the teacher?

English teachers at Jefferson High School debated this issue when it occurred to them that students might not really pick the best. Perhaps because the portfolios were to be shared among members of the department, several teachers felt they had a personal stake in the quality of their students' work. Or perhaps they were concerned that only the right papers should be submitted to the rigors of the proposed scoring process. Whatever their reasons, one department member said, "It's my job as a teacher to make sure the portfolios are an accurate reflection of what my students can do." In the end, Jefferson teachers decided that they had the *right* to choose but not enough *reason*. Not only did they want the students to own the portfolios, but they also wanted to learn from the students' choices. They believed it was valuable to know what the students valued, how they justified their selections, what standards they applied. By giving up the idea of "perfect" portfolios, Jefferson teachers ensured the portfolios would be multi-layered, packed with student-selected writing and reflections.

HOW PRECISELY SHOULD THE CONTENTS BE SPECIFIED?

Consider once more the not-so-subtle connection between portfolio purposes and contents. If the portfolio is intended to reveal the strengths and weaknesses of a particular curriculum, then its contents should reflect that curriculum. If the portfolios are to help students see themselves as authors, the contents should undoubtedly include student-devised topics and genres the students favor. But does this marriage between purpose and content mean the portfolio contents must be narrowly prescribed? What is the degree of specification for contents?

The more narrowly defined the parameters for portfolio contents, of course, the less real the selection will be. Rarely does a teacher, for example, offer students regular opportunities throughout the year to write biographies or one-act plays. If students are required to include papers in specific categories like these, chances are they will have little or no choice about the samples they pick. In contrast, if students have the opportunity to include a piece that demonstrates their skill with characterization or dialogue, they may be able to choose from among any number of pieces. Similarly, students may have a wider range of choices — and pieces for practice and revision — if they are invited to base their selections on a particular way of thinking. There is a difference between saying to students, "Pick a piece in which you evaluated or reflected on something," and saying, "Pick an evaluation paper or reflective essay." The former invites them to look for evidence of certain kinds of thinking in papers from several genres. It may make more sense to keep the content descriptions flexible so students have reasons to revise and select in order to demonstrate particular knowledge, processes or rhetorical strategies.

Many teachers, of course, simply ask for a "best" piece or pieces. Students then have the maximum say in the selection process while teachers can see how different individuals define "best" (and solve the mystery of what standards students have actually learned from writing instruction). Teachers caution, however, that "best" is different from "favorite." The former invites students to apply standards, while the latter may lead to idiosyncratic choices. Even when specifications are open-ended, they need to be deliberate.

MUST ALL THE CONTENTS BE IN A "PUBLISHABLE" STATE?

The "process-folio" is one example of portfolios that contain multiple drafts, working notes and other historical scraps. To ensure the presence of scraps, some teachers simply tell students to include one piece that shows process. Daily writing, logs, diaries, quick sketches — these, too, have their place in a portfolio if they provide the kind of information teachers and students want.

WHAT CAN STUDENTS LEARN

FROM REFLECTING?

Reflection questions should not be set in stone.

Mary Ellen Mays

I can tell by the letter, by the voice of the letter, whether the students understand what it is they are doing. The clue is how the students present themselves.

Sofia Close

In his sophomore year, Ron Cabiltes again filled his portfolio with the writings he chose as most representative of his efforts. This time his selections concentrated more on writing about ideas than on personal experience. At the end of the year, Ron's teacher asked him to look carefully through the two years of work in his portfolio and compare his first-year writings with the pieces he'd done as a sophomore. The expectation, of course, was that Ron would see improvement. He did not, however. This is what he said:

Was that really me who wrote those papers?! I can't believe it! My writing style has changed so much within the last year or so! Back then I was so descriptive, with a little humor added to my work to liven things up! But now, I think I'm more serious about what I write and to read it is like a rainy, Sunday morning with no electricity at all while your friends are out. In other words, it's BORING.

I now see why Mr. Cotton and Ms. Garamendi encourage me to write. I am good. Well, used to be. After reading my past "literature" and my present, I promise to you, Ms. Garamendi and myself, I'll change my style of writing until it is both pleasing to one's mind as well as to her/his senses. I will write the best stuff anybody has ever seen! But, I'll start tomorrow. This paper turned out to be boring also.

Here Ron presents a standard for good writing. Writing about ideas, he says, need not be devoid of voice and pizzazz. Stating that standard in his own words, Ron pledges to please the reader in the future, the key being what he calls "style."

Given the opportunity to reflect on their writing, students are capable of sophisticated observations and bald truths. They are also capable, many of them, of taking charge of their own writing. Ron, for one, can certainly decide what to do next as a writer. He possesses the data — a folder of his chosen pieces — he needs to engage in this kind of analysis.

A writer's ability to evaluate her or his writing is, according to Thomas L. Hilgers in his article, "How Children Change as Critical Evaluators of Writing," ". . . the cornerstone upon which rest the successful writer's composing skills. This is true whatever the age of the writer and whatever the writer's definition of success. Four-year-old Courtney will scowl, perhaps erase, and then try again if the figure created on paper does not match the figure of E which she carries in her head and which she is trying to recreate. Eighteen-year-old Robert, working for the summer away from home, will run to the mailbox with his letter to Anne if, when he finishes writing it, he says to himself, 'That's just what I wanted to say and just how I wanted to say it.' And whether fifty-year-old published author Lucille will revise her manuscript yet again will depend upon whether, after rereading her words, she can say, 'That'll grab 'em.'"

The key to this kind of self-evaluation is guidance from the teacher who helps students learn how to reflect.

How Can Teachers Encourage Reflection?

MODELING

One important way to help students learn to reflect is to provide them with regular opportunities to read and respond to each other's writing. Kathryn Howard, an eighth-grade teacher in Pittsburgh, encourages writers and readers to question each other:

— Writer to reader: "What did you like about the piece?" "What in the piece would you like to know more about?"

Two student writers reread favorite pieces.

— Reader to writer: "What were you thinking about when you wrote that particular sentence or paragraph?"

To ensure that student responses are substantial, rather than superficial, Howard says she "learned to model these questions often, both the phrasing and intonation, because the whole notion of talking to one another about their writing was, for my students, in some respects, new and threatening, challenging them in unfamiliar ways to accept responsibility for and ownership of their writing. Modeling response helped to establish a classroom climate in which students could freely express their feelings about their own writing and that of others because such feelings were positively channeled."

Other authors and teachers such as Donald Murray, Mary K. Healy, Marian Mohr, Rebekah Caplan, Nancie Atwell, Dan Kirby, Tom Liner, Chris Anson and Thomas Newkirk have contributed other valuable options for student-to-student response and for teaching students to respond to writing. Here is a compilation of questions designed to engage students in conversation about their writing:

1. How did you get started on this piece of writing?
2. Did you write fluently or in spurts? Explain.
3. Were you caught up in the writing or did you find it hard to concentrate? Explain.

4. Did you have enough time?
5. Did you have enough support to begin and sustain your writing?
6. Did your topic emerge quickly? Why or why not?
7. What kind of pre-writing preparation did you do?
8. At what pace did you write?
9. Did you reread what you wrote or just keep going?
10. Did you take any wrong turns or come to any halts? Explain.
11. If so, what did you do?
12. Did you revise?
13. If you wrote more than one draft, how did the paper change?
14. Did you write for a particular audience?
15. If you did have a particular audience in mind, did it make a difference to your writing?
16. How important was this writing to you?
17. Did you accomplish what you set out to do? Explain.
18. Do you have any writing rituals or routines? Explain.
19. What have you learned about yourself as a writer and about writing?

Modeling can also show students how to make their questions specific to the writing at hand. Roberta Camp, consultant to the Arts PROPEL Project, suggests that certain questions — "What did you want to get across in this piece?" or "What did you want your reader to get out of reading this piece?" — help student writers realize that each piece of writing has a purpose and a point. In this climate, student writers can also ask direct questions of their partners or response groups: "How can I get this point across?" In collaboration with teachers in the Pittsburgh schools, Camp has developed a schema that moves students from reflecting on single pieces of writing to reflecting on entire portfolios.

Reflecting on Single Pieces of Writing

Students begin by practicing reflection and making critical judgments on single pieces of writing, including trial selections for their portfolios. Camp's questions help students think about what they're learning:

— Why did you select this particular piece of writing?
— What do you see as the special strengths of this work?

— What was especially important to you during the process of writing this piece?
— What have you learned about writing from your work on this piece?
— Is there a particular technique or interest that you would like to try out or investigate further in future pieces of writing as a result of your work on this piece? If so, what is it?
— If you could go on working on this piece, what would you do?
— Was this a successful example of what you were trying out?
— How might what you learned in writing this piece affect your writing of other pieces?
— Is there anything about this piece that is still puzzling or intriguing to you — anything else you are interested in learning about?

In practicing reflection, students can also think about the processes involved in writing:

— Where did you get your idea (or ideas) for this piece?
— How did you work on it? Describe the stages the piece went through, when and where you wrote, and roughly how long each stage took.
— What kinds of changes did you make?
— What part of the process was hardest for you?
— What was easiest?
— Did you share your writing with someone else to get their ideas about it? If so, how did this sharing change the way you looked at the piece?
— Did you ever get stuck when you were writing this piece? If so, what did you do?
— How is the process you went through with this piece like the way you usually work on your writing?
— How is it different?
— How did you know that this piece was finished?

Reflecting on a Body of Work

After providing opportunities for students to reflect on single pieces of writing, teachers ask them to select two representative pieces and compare them with work done on other occasions:

— What in these pieces is like what you see in other pieces of your writing?
— What in these pieces is different from what you see in other pieces of your writing?
— What do these pieces show about you as a writer?
— What is most important to you about each of these pieces?

From here, students move to reflecting on an entire collection of work. As they examine several pieces of writing, they set goals for themselves as writers:

— After looking at these pieces, what do you think you might want to work on next in your writing?

Students also examine their portfolios — both early and later selections — to see how they have changed as writers:

— In what ways do these pieces illustrate what you can do as a writer?
— What do you notice when you look at your earlier work?
— How do you think your writing has changed?
— At what points did you discover something new about writing?
— How do the changes you see in your writing affect the way you see yourself as a writer?
— Are there any pieces you have changed your mind about over time — any that you liked before but don't like now, or any that you didn't like before but do like now? If so, which ones?
— What made you change your mind about these pieces?
— In what ways do you think your reading has influenced your writing?

If they are to learn to reflect, students need to approach it gradually with lots of support. A sequential approach, like that set out in Camp's schema, helps students become "well-equipped to monitor their own development as writers." We're not suggesting, of course, that these questions, or any others, are inviolable or appropriate for plunking in front of students with instructions that all of them must be answered. Rather, Camp's schema is a starting point for teachers who want to develop their own procedures for encouraging reflection and self-assessment. Her questions provide a framework from which other, perhaps more pertinent, questions will arise. Self-evaluation procedures are more meaningful if they are integrated into the students' continuing classroom experience.

REFLECTING ON PROCESS AND PROGRESS

University of Central Florida's Dan Kirby uses reflective questions to help students monitor the processes they go through — and the progress they make — as writers, readers and thinkers. In their book, *Mind Matters: Teaching for Thinking*, he and Carol Kuykendall describe a weekly "audit" he collects from each student:

Portfolio Audit

Do some serious rummaging around in your portfolio. Give me a freewrite report on what shape all that stuff is in. Answer the following questions honestly, please:

- What's in stock? How many pieces do you have and in what shape are they?
- What's on "back order"? What's still in your head? What pieces are you thinking about and planning to write?
- Which pieces are working? Do you have any really solid pieces that may grow into longer ones? Do you have pieces you're thinking about elaborating on?
- How are your work habits? How much time are you spending on your writing? Are you jotting notes? Working at the computer? Reading?
- What problems are you having with the writing? Is there anything I can do to help?
- Is your log up to date? Have you read the excerpts and responded to them?

These regular audits, along with post-product analyses, fit into a three-section portfolio that includes:

- Logs: Written responses to text excerpts read in class.
- Writing: The students' own pieces of writing, along with all "brainstormings and doodles and lists," written on

"restaurant napkins and backs of envelopes and yellow stickies."

— Reflections: Writing completed in response to questions about how the work is going.

Kirby says, "A carefully maintained portfolio allows both student and teacher to monitor practice, to retrace processes and to reflect on decision-making."

REFLECTING ON REVISION

University of Minnesota's Richard Beach makes revision the purpose for student reflection. Before they meet with him in conferences, students divide their drafts into sections and answer the following questions:

Describing

1. What are you trying to say or show in this section?
2. What are you trying to do in this section?
3. What are some specific characteristics of your audience?
4. What are you trying to get your audience to do or think?
5. How would you describe your organization or type of writing?
6. How would you describe your own role or orientation?

Judging

7. What are some problems you perceive in achieving 1, 2, and 4?

Selecting Appropriate Revisions

8. What are some changes you can make to deal with these problems?

Beach argues that students need help when learning how to break away from "blind allegiance" to what they think the teacher wants or to rules they may have found in composition handbooks. By modeling the kinds of questions students should ask themselves, he helps them learn how to look back on what they're doing and why.

REFLECTING ON PAST AND FUTURE WRITING

Pam Benedetti, a teacher at Elk Grove High School in California, wants to help students delve into their personal histories as readers and writers. When they submit their portfolios, they answer questions that encourage reflection such as:

— What is your history of reading and writing?
— What are your earliest memories of reading and writing?
— How did you feel about reading and writing then?
— How do you feel about it now?
— What happened in between?

Benedetti also asks her students to look forward, to set goals for themselves as writers in the future. This kind of approach to reflection emphasizes growth and development, including changing attitudes.

REFLECTING WITH AFTERWORDS AND FOREWORDS

Teachers at Jefferson High School ask their students to write afterwords as they finish each piece of writing. In the afterword, students describe what they intended to do in the piece. Student Lourdes Cuesico, for example, explains her one-act play, "Pluto's Bar and Grill in Hell" this way:

A wonderful, hilarious but fictitious play that I created which features the growing rivalry of two men about a certain lady. Included are metaphors that pertain to the real hell itself.

This afterword, which shows the influence of modern-day movie reviews, also has the advantage of providing the reader of her portfolio with a context for the entry. Afterwords, of course, can take many forms. Students might as easily write about what they've done well, what they might still change about the piece, what risks they took.

Forewords also provide orientation for portfolio readers while giving student writers the opportunity to set each piece off with a distinctive statement about its intentions, merits or features. For each piece in his portfolio, Ron Cabiltes, for example, provides a separate, brief introduction that notes the assignment as well as the reason for its selection:

We were to write an essay about a particular problem Richard Wright had as a child enclosed within his autobiography and relate it to our own life.

I chose to include this paper because this was the first time I admitted that discrimination is a part of my life. I never wanted to accept it until now.

Similarly, Roland Mackenzie introduces his play, "Mac's Life," by describing what his teacher, Mr. King, asked the class to write. Roland, however, explains that, in this case, he chose not to follow instructions. His foreword, then, becomes integral to understanding both the piece and the student writer. It reveals that Roland has the confidence and ambition to take on a new genre and a mixture of fact and fiction, past and future.

This was another assignment for English. I was told to write about my life as a play. I guess Mr. King had the idea after we read Wilder's Our Town.

I was supposed to dedicate an act to what my reflections would have been after my death, but I decided not to; instead I just made up something I believed would be just as good, looking ahead 10 years.

Most of the play is fact; only the end is fiction. I consider it my most imaginative writing because I had to picture things as they would happen, and had happened and describe thenm in a playwright's style.. As most of my writing is storytelling in nature, it took some imagination and creativity for me to finish the play.

REFLECTIVE LETTERS

Once the portfolio is assembled, students can write an introductory letter that reflects on the portfolio itself, on any of the various pieces in the portfolio or on the writer. At Miami University, for example, students receive the following instructions: "This letter, addressed to Miami University writing teachers, introduces the student and the portfolio. It may describe the process used in creating any one portfolio piece, discuss important choices in creating the portfolio, explain the place of writing in the student's life, or use a combination of these approaches. The letter should provide readers with a clearer understanding of the student as writer."

Indeed, the introductory letter is an opportunity for students to view themselves as writers, not in the abstract, but in relation to a body of work they are presenting. Kathyrn Howard asks her eighth graders to examine their final portfolios and "reflect on how you have grown and/or changed as a writer during the school year. Conclude with a paragraph evaluating your strengths and weaknesses as a writer as you prepare to enter ninth grade." Reflective letters can offer qualitative data that describe what — and how — students have learned, the writing they value and why they value it, the questions they have and the problems they've encountered — and solved — both in their classwork and beyond the familiar scope of school assignments.

In her reflective letter, eleventh-grade student Jennifer Smalley describes her progress as a writer, from changes in her attitude towards writing to improvement in her fluency. She highlights her best piece, chosen because of its personal significance and because the process of writing it enlightened and moved her. It's worth noting that Jennifer's introduction to this piece, like any good introduction, entices the reader.

Dear Reader,

It took many years for me to enjoy writing. Actually, to tell you the truth, I hated writing for years. I hated it because I had to do it to get a good grade.

When I was younger, for example in 8th grade, my writing was different. We were always given a topic to write about. Now in eleventh grade we're given a topic and learn different perspectives of writing it. I'll give an example. We had to write about Huck Finn in a situation. But you see, we had to write it so the reader is listening to Huck Finn.

The reason I hated writing was also because it seemed I couldn't think of enough information. I don't have a problem anymore. Today I think of too much and get tired of writing it all down. After all these years of writing my imagination has expanded and my grammar and punctuation has improved.

It's easier for me to write in a corner of a quiet room. When I'm thinking about what I'm going to write I don't like to be interupted because I lose my train of thought. I'd also like to add that the length of writing on my papers has has expanded. I remember when I used to have problems writing 3/4 to 1 page. Now I write one page to six pages.

My rough drafts are definitely rough. I read my rough drafts about 2 or 3 times. Each time I see something new.

The all time, best paper that I've written is my Oral History, for many reasons. The paper moved my emotions. I had interviewed my father about the Vietnam War. I never really realized what he went through until after I wrote everything down and reread it later. I cried because I didn't think it was fair that my father had to go through what he did. I took a lot of time to write it. I had a lot of patience which I had acquired within the past few years.

I think I now enjoy writing. It's a way of expressing my feelings. But I'd like to say, I don't like to write every day.

Reflection, of course, happens in many guises. This young man, introducing his portfolio to an audience of English teachers, lays out all the activities that are competing for his time. Writing is not one of them.

Dear Reader,

This folder contains some of the very finest works of literature. Well, to me it is. I'm Zandro Bermejo and I'm a junior who is very involved in a lot of activities. I'm the class vice president, I play football, basketball, and run track, all my classes are college preparatory, and a member of clubs such as CSF, Model UN, GATE, Track Club, and Basketball Club. Considering all this, you the reader should be amazed of what I have written. They are not to the best of my ability because as you can see, I'm too involved in too many things. But they're still great because it was written by someone great. (as you can see, great wasn't capitalized meaning I'm not conceited.)

Enjoy my writing. They express a lot about me and my character. Again let me remind you that I can write better than this. I added an extra paper which was an incident in my life. It was with my friends. Don't criticize too much because as one of my mottos say, "There's too many damn critics in this world!"

Zandro

Zandro is an immigrant student. One of the pieces in his portfolio describes his plane trip to America. "I thought of all the friends I left behind," he writes. "They were all poor and I knew they'd rather be in my shoes." Indeed, his shoes are very busy and when it comes time to reflect, he reveals he has not met his own expectations as a writer. In fact, his portfolio does not demonstrate any kind of gradual progress. Some of his early writings are more effective than pieces written later in the year when his other commitments were at their most pressing. So the letter of introduction is crucial to Zandro's teachers; it gives them a context for evaluating the portfolio. They can acknowledge that Zandro barely held his own as a writer because he had other important things to do. "As teachers, we must listen first to the perceptions our students have of themselves," says Linda Rief of New Hampshire's Oyster River Middle School. Ultimately, she says, students show us who they are "as readers, writers, thinkers and human beings."

SETTING GOALS

Rief sees student reflection in terms of goal-setting. She encourages students to argue in favor of the best piece in their portfolios and compare it to the least effective. Then they turn to their goals:

— What goals did you set for yourself?
— How well did you accomplish them?
— What are your goals for the next 12 weeks?

When you must hand out grades, says Rief, "Base the grade on goals set and achieved as evidenced in the portfolio of only (the students') best work."

Open-ended questions like those Rief poses encourage students to reflect on their long-term as well as immediate goals for writing. Reflecting on a single piece of writing leads naturally to thinking about immediate goals; for example, specific revisions. But if teachers ask students to reflect on their personal goals in relation to writing collected over a span of time, they are encouraging students to set goals for their own development as writers. Both kinds of reflection are valuable.

What Do Reflections Tell Teachers?

Student reflections help teachers answer what Roberta Herter, in her article, "Writing Portfolios: Alternatives to Testing," describes as the "subtle questions which inform the teaching of writing: What processes underlie changes in writing and attitudes toward writing? What kinds of writing give full voice to student thinking? How does time affect the process?"

Student Richelle Pena, for example, reflects on the conditions that make a difference to her writing:

The way I write best is when I'm alone and there is no noice around me . . . also the best time when I could write is at nite when I'm reflecting on the things I've done during the day, but I can't write them down because I just can't get up and turn on the light because my sister would kill me.

With improper conditions as one barrier to success and a set of school assignments as another, Richelle expresses disappointment in her portfolio:

I don't really like what's in my portfolio, because well, there are only about 3 of the 5 stories please me, the other 2 I don't like them because the subjects weren't interested to me, they were things I HAD to do and not ones I WANTED to.

Her classmates at a California urban middle school agree that mandatory topics are a detriment. Andrew writes, for example, "I don't like writing on a set topic because it may be a topic I don't like," while Robin says, ". . . how much control you have over what you can write can make a difference."

Gwen, an English as a second language student, addresses the subtle question of time in her introductory letter:

. . . the writing I do in class will never be better or more interested than the ones I do at home. Writing on my spare time is to me without pressure of time due, or a bad grade. That way, I feel more comfortable, and my writing would just flow through.

Classmate Vernon takes issue with particular classroom activities that are not useful to him as a writer: "When I write, I don't begin by mapping or brainstorming; mapping is too much trouble for something that doesn't help me at all."

In other words, student reflections give teachers information about the circumstances and the interventions that help or hinder students' writing. If they didn't ask, how else would teachers find out?

Student Reflection: Issues and Concerns

WHEN IS REFLECTION JUST ANOTHER VERSION OF DRILL AND KILL?

It is possible to teach reflection as the five-paragraph essay or any other formula for writing. Any kind of fill-in-the-blanks approach to reflection is antithetical to the nature of reflection and to the purpose of having students look closely at what they do. Certainly, the questions outlined earlier in this chapter could be transformed into worksheets. Letters, too, can belie teachers' best intentions. Some California teachers, for example, have tried to structure reflection by giving students a format for the letters. Their students, sensitive and dutiful about doing exactly what school asks them to do, turn their reflections into mechanical, orderly responses to teacher-posed prompts. Even the simplest directions — "Tell why you picked each piece for your portfolio" — can produce a reflective letter that sounds like a table of contents. The point is that students need guidance and practice with, not a workbook approach to, reflection.

To help students feel at ease with the "not- precisely-what-I-say" approach to reflection, Mt. Diablo High School's Bruce White frequently asks for letters on a whole range of matters. "Write to me about why you liked a particular book," he suggests to his students on one occasion. "Persuade me to see a certain movie," he says on another, or, "Tell me why this piece of writing is your personal best." His questions have direction, but they are also open-ended. They attend to purpose and audience but leave other matters of writing to the writer. The trick is to find a balance between giving students too many cues and too few. The latter leaves students, as Miles Myers describes it, in a state of "existential nausea."

WHAT JUSTIFIES DEVOTING TIME TO REFLECTION?

Devoting class time to selection and reflection takes away from other, perhaps equally important, instruction. Arts PRO-PEL's Dennie Palmer Wolf gives us ample argument, however, for concentrating on a "portfolio culture." Culture, as Wolf uses the word, refers to an interactive classroom, one in which students reflect on their own and others' portfolios and the teacher responds to the students' portfolios and reflections. This culture benefits students by helping them become conscious of process and, therefore, increases their control of the decisions they make and their willingness to experiment. Students, in working regularly with portfolios, begin to appreciate the development of a work. They become active learners and active observers. In short, they join a community of artists and writers who set their own goals and serve as resources for each other. All this takes time.

For students, reflection is, in part, self-evaluation. When they reflect, they make judgments about the effectiveness of their writing. Mt. Diablo teacher, Maxine Emerson, for example, asks her junior students to look over their writing in earlier portfolios and to write about what they notice. One student notes, "I have learned to write for the reader." Another mourns the passing of youthful spontaneity, ". . . just the thought of being in an 'honors' class makes me tend to write in a more erudite manner. The only thing that kind of bothers me is that I seem to have lost some of the creativity that showed in some ancient papers." (Her teacher assures her that this loss is only temporary.) A classmate writes, "I get more to the point more quickly. I also see my major problem of run-a-way sentences decreasing."

Portfolios provide students with concrete demonstrations of what they can do. In the absence of concrete writing, reflections are simply memories, a recounting of old attitudes and associations. Reflections that accompany writings, on the other hand, make direct references to real work, real criteria and the real circumstances in which papers were produced. "I notice the improvement of my vocabulary," junior Carol Richter writes proudly. Paul, on the other hand, finds his portfolio from the previous year filled with demons:

I was taken back to a time when I was very negative and found a perverse happiness in telling life from my twisted point of view. Why was I not locked up in a mental institute? I seemed dark and deranged in those days.

The argument that students are too young or too inexperienced to make something of their portfolios simply does not hold. In each of the previous cases, students have become, through reflection, more conscious of their growth as writers and even their progress as human beings. They address for themselves the question that plagues so many students during their school careers — "So what?"

. . . .

WHEN FOLDERS ARE FILLED —

WHAT NEXT?

Portfolios help make teachers comfortable as kid watchers and kid evaluators.

John Winbury

Portfolios give students the opportunity to evaluate themselves and to set the standards of good writing.

Bob Ingalls

When Ron Cabiltes submitted his portfolio to the English department at Mt. Diablo High School, he may have expected a grade or score from his evaluators. Instead, he received a full-page letter responding to his portfolio and to him as a writer. His teachers, when they thrashed out how to handle the completed portfolios, remained true to their original purposes, one of which was to motivate the students as writers. It followed, then, that writers deserve to hear from their readers, not in terms of marks, but in terms of honest reactions. The teachers wrote to Ron and his classmates about what they liked in the portfolios, what they saw as the writers' strengths, and what they thought each should consider next, whether that was to try a new direction or to aim for improvement in a specific area.

These were not easy letters to write. Teachers had to learn a completely new way of responding to their students. They were used to the assignment-by-assignment method. They were not used to fanning out the papers of one writer and responding in terms of questions they had about the whole of a writer's work and work strategies:

— How does this writer fare across different kinds of writing or writing done for different audiences and purposes?

— How does this writer solve the problems that writers solve?
— How does this writer manage a process?
— In what ways and to what extent has this writer changed and progressed?
— What are this writer's strengths? Weaknesses? Special talents?
— How does this student assess him or herself and by what standards?

Let's look at one teacher's letter to Ron:

Dear Ron,

Your portfolio is a delight! It showed that you are aware of your reader and you take care of your reader. For example, your presentation of the portfolio worked well: table of contents, introductory letter, short introduction to each piece, dated papers. I found the collection easy to follow and I felt you were guiding me to the features of your writing that pleased and concerned you.

The outstanding feature of your writing for me is the imagery. The way you described your feelings of boredom — "like a rainy Sunday morning with no electricity at all while your friends are out" — is anything but boring! You observe closely, Ron, and often you find the irony in things. For example, in your monologue of a snake, when the snake owner releases the snake in the wild, you observe: "There were no specially prepared foods in the wilderness, unlike the glass home I so loved." Look at the pieces in your portfolio that bored you. I think you'll find, particularly in the sketch of your mother, that the sharp details, metaphors and pictures are missing. Compare those pieces with the ones that pleased you.

How much do you revise your work? I know I have to write several drafts before I'm satisfied. My impression from looking at the drafts you included in your portfolio is that you've made few changes. I'd like to see you dig in next year and tackle revision. For example, the piece on your mother deserves a second or third round. You want to add examples and incidents for statements like, "She stands strong when troubles occur."

I know you can tuck incidents into your pieces. That's just what you did in the Black Boy paper to illustrate your own bout with discrimination. How would that technique have worked in your other responses to literature? It seems a new technique for you, one you didn't use so much last year. I'd say you've progressed and you should take advantage of what you've learned to do so well.

I'm glad to know that you enjoyed all the writing you did for this portfolio, Ron. Yes, I thoroughly enjoyed reading it and I look forward to what comes next.

For Ron and his classmates, these letters were stunning to receive. Mt. Diablo students were not used to reading about themselves as writers nor were they used to having their writing read by an adult other than their own teacher. (Mt. Diablo teachers were careful to respond to the portfolios of students who were not in their classes.) Here are some excerpts showing what students had to say to the teachers who read and responded to their portfolios:

Thank you very much for the encouraging complements and constructive criticism. I will work on the pieces you suggested, especially the memory writing and the "Car I'd invent." Over the summer I'm going to work on a book that tells my life-story, but very, very exaggerated. I'll have to think up some new names for everyone involved but it shouldn't be too hard. If I get you for English II, I hope you wouldn't mind proofreading it.

I have recive your letter today, on my final day. Before I recive this letter, I said to myself, "Oh no, I hope someone who read my portfolio like it." Because this is my first time doing this, and I'm not sure what I write in this is right. When I recive this letter. I was so happy that you like it. I think I'm going to imporve my organizing on writing in paragraphs next year. Thank you for take your time to read this.

I would like to inform you that God does exist because I prayed that you would be the one to read my refeshing and lucid writing. And he answered my prayers. Amen.

I'm pleased to hear your response to my literature.

What these excerpts reveal is that students, particularly those for whom English is a second language, can be somewhat anxious about portfolio evaluation. At the same time, they are eager to establish a writer-to-reader relationship with their evaluators and to commit to making specific improvements. Many students, like the young man who wrote the last comment, see their work as literature. Indeed, portfolios can elevate students' views of themselves, particularly if the evaluation process recognizes the literary merit of student writing.

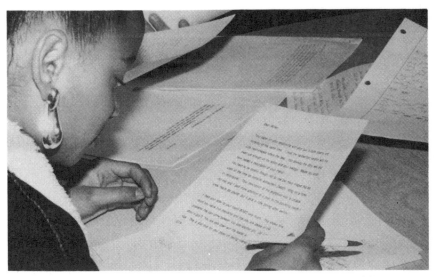

A writer reads a letter from a teacher who reviewed her portfolio.

Letters from teachers have a different effect from a grade or score. Letters treat students as authors while grades or scores do not. Letters instruct and qualify; they do not rank or categorize. Letters are personal; grades or scores are not. Whether the feedback is provided through a letter or other similar means, there needs to be useful feedback that helps students learn.

The Value of Analysis

ALICE TRAN'S PORTFOLIO

Alice Tran's portfolio contains two pieces of particular interest to her teacher. One is her "idea paper," a response to Richard Wright's book, *Black Boy*. Short and full of bland generalizations, it contains statements like, "Experience is not something that can be given to you," and "Richard Wright has gained a vast education on human rights." Alice's teacher longs for a single detail, one solid example. Then the teacher finds Alice's personal experience paper. It goes like this:

Ever since I was a child, I have always felt the need to fit in with the American crowd. Just to be normal; not Asian. Over the years, I slowly began to lose my language as well as my culture. I blamed my parents for not being Americans. I didn't want to be the person that stuck out in the crowd. All my friends had blond and brown hair and I had black. I began to only speak English at home. My parents seemed oblivious to the fact that I was losing my heritage. When I was in the seventh grade, I began my changing process. I seemed to see everything through different eyes. My parents finally forced me to become involved in the Vietnamese choir even though I was illiterate. I tried to sing along, memorizing half the words because I couldn't read them. After along time, I was able to read without having the songs memorized beforehand. Through the choir, I learned to understand and appreciate my heritage again.

Many people don't realize the advantages of being bilingual until it is too late. I was caught between two cultures that were a world apart. The only way I could have both was by understanding and appreciating my own first.

The teacher and Alice place this paper and the response to *Black Boy* side by side. They compare the level of detail, the number of generalizations, the progression in each paper. They agree that Alice has developed valuable strategies to draw on, strategies that she can use in any number of writing situations and could have used in her response to Wright's book.

Then they talk about what happens when Alice works from experience into idea. Experience and ideas go together, they decide. They decide this on the basis of real data because they are looking at one paper that includes experience and one that leaves it out altogether. Their analysis will make a difference to Alice's future performance. She will be more conscious of writing strategies and how they can be transferred from paper to paper.

Portfolios invite analysis. One group of teachers analyzes portfolios by writing letters to students. Another group uses portfolios in regular teacher-student conferences or in interactions between students. To ignore analysis is to ignore the potential of portfolios.

Analysis is difficult in traditional situations when teachers must read papers by the bundle, one assignment after another. As they sift through a veritable tower of papers, all by different student authors, they are limited to learning something about the tower itself and the comparative writing skills of the class in a particular situation. The alternative is portfolio analysis, a horizontal reading of papers from the same student to see how that student fares in many different writing situations. The primary focus is now the student rather than the assignment. The picture is no longer finite; it's infinite. And the teacher's thoughtful comments to students like Alice are not just endings. They're also beginnings.

FRANCIE CHOY'S PORTFOLIO

Francie, a ninth grader, is participating in a writing-across-the-curriculum portfolio project. She selects pieces for her final portfolio from work done in several of her classes. Her teachers want to see how Francie and her classmates fare in different writing situations where purposes and audiences for writing vary widely. Further, the teachers intend to look at how their students manage various writing processes, particularly revision. Finally, they want to examine the school-wide writing program. Let's look through the major part of Francie's portfolio with these three purposes in mind. Her introductory letter begins the portfolio:

Dear Reader,

My favorite writing piece I chose was "My First Kiss." I like this piece because it showed good dialogue, with enough description to show how I was feeling. It also had some humor in it, which is good.

"My First Kiss" is an example of what I'm good at. I'm considerably good at using dialogue and using description for my emotions. I figure I'm good at this because I have a broad range of emotions to choose from. My weakness in writing is writing rough drafts, because I don't see the point in it. I'm also weak at rewriting long drafts because I get really restless. When I get restless I watch T.V. and I may never stop. That's bad.

The method that I use for writing is I go to my living room, turn on the radio, and get cracking. The music helps me write. I don't know why, but the faster the music, the faster I write. I hate it when people are around me when I write. I don't know why, I guess I'm independent.

The type of writing I do best is narrative writing. I guess I like to write this way because I like telling stories and am good at making people understand how I feel.

Sincerely,

Francie Choy

Francie is a delight to her teachers. They immediately appreciate her sense of audience, the clear indications that she wants to appeal to her readers. This introductory letter gives them a frame of reference for the entire portfolio. Francie sees her strength as "using dialogue and using description" in narrative writing, allowing her to work with the reader to "understand how I feel." However, she finds revision pointless. It makes her "restless" and sends her running to the television for relief. She seems to value a speedy pen that becomes speedier with the beat of the music. Is it fair to guess that Francie finds the most virtue in "doneness"? Will the portfolio show that Francie is an impatient reviser?

My First Kiss

"You have to do it sometime," I thought for at least the 500th time.

My heart was pounding louder than a drum, playing with the upmost strength.

"Oh my god!" I chided with myself. "Just press your lips against his and hold on till you lose your breath. Than pull back. You can do it."

Another voice in my scrambled brain said, "You mother would never approve!!"

"So?", said another voice in my silly brain, "So what. Who cares what mom thinks? It's my life!"

"Hi!" said my boyfriend, interrupting my thoughts.

"Hi," I said listlessly.

"Is anything wrong?" He asked.

"What? Oh, nothing's wrong. Oh come on! Let's get it over with!"

"Gee, you're SOOOOO enthusiastic!!" he said in this really, I repeat really sarcastic way.

I felt as though I was talking to an enemy. "Listen, I want it. You want it. So let's get it over with, OKAY??!!!"

"Okay!!," he said, mad. Then he said gently, "Let's not fight"

"Okay." I whispered.

He drew closer and closer to me. We were just a teeny inch from kissing. I drew back while he fell back, startled.

"What?" he stammered, "Why?"

"I'm scared..." I said shaking.

"Scared!?," he said surprised.

"Yeah, I've never done it before," I said close to tears.

"You haven't! Gosh, well ...uh," he fumbled.

"But I want to, okay?", I said weakly.

"Allright...!", he said, smiling, his brilliant eyes dancing.

He pulled closer to me, and I wrapped my arms around his neck. While his lips were just a milimeter from mine, I shivered.

Finally, he put his lips tenderly on mine. I held on, just swept away, as he was. Then we pulled back. We breathed.

I'll always remember my first kiss.

The End

Francie shows that, indeed, she's a confident writer of dialogue. She creates a whole scene — with beginning, middle and end — relying solely on the conversation between two characters. It's no small accomplishment, either, that Francie successfully punctuates all the talk. Her teachers agree that "My First Kiss" is a little gem, written with real readers in mind.

Francie's second portfolio selection, an imaginary letter home written by a soldier during the American Civil War, is from her social studies class.

Dear Mom and Dad,

Hello, John here, sending you a message, that I am thank God, alive and well. I guess "well" is not the word that I should describe on how I feel. I don't want to die, I don't want to miss out on Dad's 50th birthday, or Mom's 48th birthday. I miss Teddy and his innocent, wonderful self. How old is he now? Two? Three?

Everyday, when we head towards another battle that lasts for eons, I dread the blow of a gun. Whenever I kill a soldier, (this is bad) but I feel terrible, knowing I killed someone with a productive life before the war. It is scary to think my fighting will result the fate of the Union. I sometimes lay awake at night, praying to God to keep me alive till tomorrow and until I could say hello to you guys. I miss you all so much. I will fight with my last ounce of courage to come home. That is my goal. Good-bye for now, 'till I see you.

I MISS YOU

Missing the comfort of Home,

John

Francie's teachers immediately recognize the sincere tone of this letter. They appreciate Francie's efforts in trying to capture the pain of battle. However, the Civil War is far removed from the experience of a 14-year-old girl. Francie runs into trouble when she attempts to adopt the persona of a soldier. Her character's loyalties, other than those to his family, remain a mystery in this piece. Francie's reader has no clue about North or South, let alone the soldier's whereabouts or the circumstances in which he has been forced to kill. The letter might have been written during any war, by any soldier from any country. It also lacks a story and storytelling is one of Francie's strengths as a writer.

On the following two pages, reproduced as Francie wrote them in her English class, are the first draft and later revision of a review of the TV program, *Doogie Howser, M.D.*, written in the form of a letter to the actor who plays Doogie.

This review is full of generalities, unembellished by the dialogue and description Francie recognizes as features of her best writing. In spite of all her enthusiasm for the show, Francie limits herself to a string of adjectives — funny, interesting, great, insightful, fantastic, cool, cute. The reader has no notion of the qualities that entitle the show to this praise. Indeed, Francie seems to have forgotten about the reader altogether in this piece, not to mention Doogie, who might like to know exactly what pleases.

This portfolio entry also speaks to Francie's disclaimers about revision. Her teachers see few changes between the first and second drafts of the piece. Francie did set herself up to revise by writing on every other line of her first draft. Her response partner, however, made few suggestions ("Good, I think it's great too!" and "I don't think you need it.") and Francie was evidently satisfied as well. The teachers speculate that Francie either misunderstood revision, equating it with recopying, had never learned how to revise or simply saw no reason for doing so.

Finally, here's Francie's science selection, another letter.

Dear Demi,

Hi, what's up? Today in Science, we did a fun experiment. The problem of the lab was to see if we could tell whether a liquid did or did not have acids in it.

First, Mrs. O'Donnell handed out Litmus paper. This is a paper that changes colors as a reaction of an acid. There were also liquids (i.e. water, ammonia, lemon juice, HCL, unknown, tomatoe juice, and shampoo.) We took this stuff and dropped it on the Litmus paper.

Frances Fong

Dear Neil (a.k.a. Doogie),
 Hi & My name is ~~Frances~~ Fong, and I would like to tell you, your show is one of my most favorite. I keep Wednesday night at 9:00 always open to watch you. Are you really as serious as you seem? How old are you really?

 Your show is really funny, as well as interesting. You give kids a positive image, that its cool to achieve high standards. I think that's great! * Good, I think it's great too!

 One of your shows, (the one where you were planning to have sex w/ wanda) was very insightful. You showed exactly what goes on w/ teenagers today. You also show that it's better not to rush sex and to wait a while. That's fantastic, and it makes people think —
 I don't think you need it.

 Your friend Vinnie, is really cool, too. He adds humor to the show. ~~brings you your liveliness. And wanda, well she's weird.~~

 All of your show's have meaning, and ~~you~~ make that happen. I also love it, ~~after~~ when you type in your computer. That sumons everything up, and ~~gives~~ makes everything have a good point.
 Stay cute & and keep on acting.

 P.S. ~~████~~   Love your fan,
                              ~~Frances Fong~~
                              Frances Fong

Wild card
~~Portfolio~~

Frances Fong
English - 04
Ms. Harris
May 15, 1990

Dear Neil (a.k.a. Doogie Howser),

Hi ! My name is Frances Fong, and I would like to tell you, your show is one of my most favorite. I keep Wednesday night at 9:00 always open to watch you. Are you really as serious as you seem? How old are you really?

Your show is really funny, as well as interesting. You give kids a positive image it's cool to achieve high standards. I think that's great 8 %

One of your shows (the one where Doogie plans to have sex with Wanda) was very insightful. You showed people exactly what goes on with teens today. That's fantastics, and it makes people think.

Your friend Vinnie is really cool, too. He adds humor to the show.

All of your shows have meaning, and you make that happen. I also love it when you type on your computer. That sums up everything, and makes everything have a point. Stay cute and keep on acting.

Love, your fan 4-ever
Francis Fong

If the liquid was an acid, it would change to pink. If it was not an acid, it would stay blue. (original color) This part was very fun.

My hypothesis was wrong. Ammonia did NOT have acid. I thought it did. Did you know water had acid in it? I didn't. I really did not know shampoo had acids in it. Did you? Once I placed shampoo on the thin paper, it automatically turned bright pink! Wow!!

One error I made was I mixed up the litmus paper, and forgot which acid was which! What a mess! Next time, I will be more careful. So what? You're probably thinking! Well basically I'm trying to say is there are lots of liquids with acids in it, and you could never be too safe! Looks CAN be deceiving! I'm also saying something has got to be done about acids!

Well, I have to go. Did you have fun in Spanish? (Probably NOT!) Hasta Luego!

Love,
your now CAUTIOUS friend,
Francie

The science lab letter comes as a relief. Whether it is the familiarity of the audience or her confidence in her new-found discovery, Francie brings authority and detail to this piece. She manages some storytelling. In contrast to her two other letters, this one raises questions about the teaching and uses of writing across the school. What are the effects of audience and role-playing on student performance? Did it make a difference that, this time, Francie was writing to a close friend? Did it make a difference that she was writing to the teacher at the same time? At Francie's school, what kinds of preparation and rehearsal typically precede the drafting of a paper? Does Francie understand the expectations of each task? Are the expectations made explicit? To what extent is Francie aware of "style" in these letters as she seems to be in "The First Kiss"? To what extent is style important in different disciplines?

This is the kind of questioning that helps teachers teach. They can experiment with audience in writing to learn, as, in fact, the teachers at Francie's school did after reading and discussing cross-disciplinary portfolios. They can reinforce what students do well, including, in Francie's case, her accurate self-evaluation. They can also establish priorities. Francie's teachers made revision a teaching priority in their school-wide writing program the following year, realizing from Francie's portfolio and others (oh, the amount of recopying a 14-year- old does!) that they needed to focus their efforts.

Criteria for Evaluating Portfolios

Analyses are, of course, based on criteria. But where do the criteria come from? Are there criteria for developing criteria? Here's a loose list of suggestions:

— Criteria come from the writing itself. They are not a set of abstract rules unrelated to the intention of the writer or the writing teacher. They are set in a context; that is, clearly and directly related to particular conditions.
— Criteria are not the special property of commercial test-makers. Teachers can develop criteria. So can students.
— Criteria should be useful to the writer and to the writing teacher.
— Criteria can apply to individual pieces in the portfolio or to the portfolio as a whole.
— Criteria can be expressed in many forms. For example, they can be descriptions or they can be exemplars, papers or portfolios that exemplify certain criteria.

TWO ENGLISH DEPARTMENTS APPROACH EVALUATION

When teachers gather to discuss criteria for evaluating portfolios as they did in the Mt. Diablo High School English department, they can begin by looking at portfolios-in-progress. They can search for exemplars, model portfolios or individual pieces that demonstrate high achievement. They can also describe exactly what makes a particular folder or paper effective. And, of course, they can debate the importance of what they see. Listen to the Mt. Diablo teachers as they come to terms with a particular criterion:

"There's too much emphasis on voice in this department. Kids can write without telling all their feelings and sometimes I'd prefer they do."

"Voice isn't just telling your feelings."

"Do all assignments call for voice? Does it matter who the audience is?"

"It would be interesting to have the kids tell us who the audience is for each piece."

"They'd probably say 'the teacher.'"

This snippet of conversation illustrates several points. First, criteria need to be defined, for both teachers and students. To do so, teachers and students must take the time to talk to each other. Second, criteria, when they are dealt with in terms of real student writing, bring teachers and students right back to the work at hand and to what they are trying to accomplish. Third, criteria are of no use unless they are public property. Teachers and students benefit only when they can understand criteria, argue their value and refer to them regularly in their classroom efforts.

During the first two years of their portfolio assessment project, the Mt. Diablo English teachers applied separate criteria to each piece of writing in the portfolios. In fulfilling one of the purposes of their portfolio assessment — to examine the four-year curriculum — they found it only sensible to begin by evaluating the elements of that curriculum; specifically, different kinds of writing. They could assess narrative writing, then, by examining the student writer's ability to shape a story, to impress the reader with its significance, to write with specificity, with imagery, with metaphor. Persuasive writing called for evaluation according to different criteria: the student writer's ability to take and support a stand with evidence, facts, examples and details, and to examine an issue from other angles while winning over the reader to a particular point of view.

The advantage of this particular system is that teachers and students make legitimate and useful distinctions among genres. Each set of criteria informs a particular writing situation with its distinctive characteristics. Rather than lumping together different writing features or looking holistically at writing performance, teachers at Mt. Diablo were able to zero in on specific strengths or weaknesses in students' performances in specific writing modes. The disadvantage of this kind of evaluation is that it focuses more on individual assignments than on individual writers.

During the third year of the portfolio assessment project, Mt. Diablo teachers abandoned the paper-by-paper approach for its alternative: applying criteria to the portfolio as a whole. From the outset in September, they geared the portfolios to individual writers by asking students to include best pieces, works in progress, evidence of revision, writing across disciplines and the like. The criteria, then, became more general-ized: focus, voice, organization, development, sentence style, correctness.

The advantage of this system is that it focuses on the whole rather than the parts. It places the writers, with their idio-syncratic ups and downs, in the forefront. It allows both teachers and students to assess specific strengths or accom-plishments — as well as specific limitations or things-to-be-learned-next — across types of writing. The disadvantage is that criteria sometimes mean more when they are placed in context, anchored in specific writing situations with specific purposes.

In Virginia, members of the Mt. Vernon High School Eng-lish department offer another alternative for looking at stu-dent portfolios as a whole. They use the following scoring criteria to obtain information about individual student perfor-mance and about program:

WRITING PORTFOLIO ASSESSMENT

Check the box that best reflects student performance. Use the space provided to comment.

The portfolio has these qualities:

	most of the time			none of the time
	4	3	2	1

Versatility and Adaptability

1. Is there a variety of forms?   4__3__2__1__
2. Is there a variety of voices and purposes?   4__3__2__1__
3. Are there writings for a variety of audiences?   4__3__2__1__

Completeness

4. Is there a sustained focus?   4__3__2__1__
5. Is there coherence?   4__3__2__1__
6. Is there appropriate balance of specificity and generality?   4__3__2__1__
7. Do the forms (letters, essays, research papers, etc.) have appropriate characteristics?   4__3__2__1__

Carefulness

    8. Is there carefulness in gram-
       mar and mechanics?   4___3___2___1___

Beauty and Power

    9. Is the wording precise?
       Powerful? Beautiful?   4___3___2___1___
10. Is there a natural and effec-
       tive voice?   4___3___2___1___
11. Are the arguments or images
       moving?   4___3___2___1___

Responsibility

12. Does the student select topics
       and forms?   4___3___2___1___
13. Does the student make
       choices based on comments
       of readers?   4___3___2___1___
14. Does the student revise?   4___3___2___1___
15. Does the student edit?   4___3___2___1___

                      TOTAL   ___ ___ ___ ___

General Comments

A STATEWIDE APPROACH TO EVALUATION: VERMONT

Without easy or once-and-for-all answers to the questions of
what criteria to apply and how to apply them, teachers must
return once again to the purposes of the portfolio project.
Suppose, for example, the purpose is to find out how well both
schools and students in an entire state are doing. In undertak-
ing this staggering challenge, Vermont teachers have developed a trial set of criteria that leads reviewers from looking
at individual writers and their individual portfolios, to looking at the school's writing program. Each of the criteria is
rated at four levels.

Is the writer's purpose clear?

    Rarely ___ Sometimes ___ Frequently ___ Extensively ___

Does use of specific detail add to clarity?

    Rarely ___ Sometimes ___ Frequently ___ Extensively ___

Does the writing exhibit a sense of personal expression, voice or effective tone?

    Rarely ___ Sometimes ___ Frequently ___ Extensively ___

Does the final draft exhibit appropriate usage, mechanics and grammar?

    Rarely ___ Sometimes ___ Frequently ___ Extensively ___

In addition, reviewers will answer three questions that relate to the school's writing program:

Is there progress from earliest dated works to most recently dated works?

    Rarely ___ Sometimes ___ Frequently ___ Extensively ___

Is there evidence of sufficient variety to challenge all students and to allow each student an opportunity for success?

    Rarely ___ Sometimes ___ Frequently ___ Extensively ___

Is there evidence of teacher/peer response to the student's drafts, and is there opportunity for the student to revise?

    Rarely ___ Sometimes ___ Frequently ___ Extensively ___

Vermont teachers serve as reviewers to apply these criteria. First, they read each student's portfolio at the local school. Then they take a random sample of portfolios to a regional moderation session where additional teachers rescore the sample as a reliability check. The next step is state-level moderation, where an even smaller sample of the portfolios gets the same treatment. The moderation process takes on many of the features of a good staff development session where teachers arrive at a common view of standards based on real writing.

At this time, the Vermont portfolio program is in the pilot stage. Already, however, the advantages are apparent. The criteria are available for public discussion and teachers can apply them when they review the writing of the students in their classes. The criteria, however, in no way dictate or limit what teachers teach. They don't, for example, specify particular assignments. Further, the criteria are applied by teachers rather than reviewers outside the teaching profession. A note of caution, however. If individual students are to receive meaningful feedback about their writing, it is essential for their teachers to respond to their writing in ways that go well beyond the state scoring system. And for portfolios to contribute substantially to teaching and learning, they must integrate the purposes developed by individual teachers and students with those of the state assessment program.

A NATIONWIDE APPROACH TO EVALUATION: AP STUDIO ART

On a national level, the Advanced Placement studio art examination is a country-wide portfolio assessment that gives U. S. high school students the chance to earn college credit by examination. Every year, 4,500 students submit bulky portfolios full of drawings and pictures to Educational Testing Service (ETS), a testing company. Eventually, these portfolios make their way to a gymnasium for a two-day scoring session. Each portfolio receives three scores. Raters review the standards at the beginning of the scoring by looking at a number of portfolios that illustrate all the possible scores. The "types" — exemplars of each score — stay on display at the side of the room so that raters can consult them when they get stuck. Exemplars are crucial to portfolio assessment or, indeed, to any other kind of performance assessment. They are the flesh on the bare bones of criteria. They are the concrete reminders, the demonstrations of specific features, the visual evidence of effectiveness.

Also worth noting in this particular Advanced Placement examination is the jury method of judging works of art, where, according to Ruth Mitchell in *Performance Assessment: What It Is and What It Looks Like*, ". . . collective judgment substitutes for objectivity. The jury method is widely accepted in other fields — sports, ballet, music, and drama competitions, for example." In this case, jury members talk through disagreements over portfolios, the more experienced raters helping their less experienced colleagues compare problem portfolios with the "types." Being a juror, then, is an education in itself, a look into classrooms and learning. Portfolio assessment, when it provides the chance for negotiation, makes visible not only performances, but also the analysis of performances. It's that analysis, combined with the exemplars, that give teachers and students the wherewithal to improve what they do.

CLASSROOM APPROACHES TO EVALUATION

Dixie Dellinger's students in North Carolina place three pieces each quarter in their portfolios, selecting from persuasive pieces, personal narratives, responses to literature and poetry. Because Dellinger is already familiar with the pieces, she concentrates her evaluation — a personal letter to each student — on what the student says about the pieces. "I ask students to write reflections on each of the three writings they have chosen. They are to tell me why they chose the piece and what it shows about the student as a reader, writer, and thinker." In other words, evaluation is a shared process in Dellinger's class and an extension of other evaluation methods.

In contrast, Margie Krest grades the portfolios of the students in her Colorado high school class as well as the individual pieces in their portfolios. The portfolio grade reflects"the amount of revision, risk taking, and changing they did on all their papers." Krest grades the individual papers as final products, applying hierarchical criteria. At the high end, she looks for such features as focus, development and voice. At the low end, she is concerned with usage. It is possible, Krest acknowledges, to avoid grading individual papers and simply give the portfolio two grades: one for risk and revision; another reflecting criteria that apply to effective writing.

In Bob Ingalls' class at Mt. Vernon High School in Virginia, students grade each other's portfolios. They begin the quarter with a class discussion to set the standards for good writing. They read up to 10 portfolios to get a sense of what makes a top, mediocre and fair portfolio. The criteria, then, help shape the student writing that follows throughout the quarter. Once assembled, the portfolios — which contain students' five best pieces — are distributed among the students who score and comment on the contents. Ingalls is the final judge. The entire process, he says, gives students the opportunity to evaluate themselves and to set and apply standards. His burden is greatly lessened as well.

Writing buddies read each other's work.

Portfolios are "a natural end" in a writing class, says Jane Juska, English teacher at Ygnacio Valley High School in Concord, California. "I don't want to have a paper due each week and grade it." Students in Juska's class assemble their portfolios at the end of each quarter, introducing each piece with a cover sheet that explains how it succeeds and where it falls short. The purpose of the quarterly portfolio is to provide students with responses and direction along the way to assembling a portfolio at the end of the semester. Accordingly, in addition to the teacher, they must have one person outside the class and another inside the class respond to their portfolios.

Because these quarterly portfolios can contain works-in-progress, Juska says she focuses her comments on "where I see these pieces going." Students also focus the comments by telling Juska what they would like her to pay particular attention to in their papers. "I want to know what students are going to do with these comments," says Juska. "Will they go the way of all comments? I'm not satisfied with 'thanks a lot.' So I ask students for a letter back telling me exactly how they'll use the suggestions they've received. And one of the requirements of the semester portfolio is to include revisions based on what's been said about the quarterly portfolio."

It's worth noting that Juska experiments freely and fearlessly with portfolios, experiments that surely encourage students to do the same. In fact, she asks directly for "challenges," papers in the portfolio that demonstrate something students have never tried before.

Along with all the serious talk about what to do with portfolios, Juska reminds us that, ultimately, portfolios should please both the writer and the reader. That's why one of her experiments has been a semester portfolio that asks students to include:

— Something old (a revision).
— Something new (an experiment).
— Something a little bit borrowed (a piece inspired by another piece).
— Something blue.

By treating portfolios both playfully and seriously and by spoofing categories, Juska helps students understand that portfolios can and should be appealing, that someone should want to read them, and that evaluation is a response to something that's alive, not dead.

Certain intangible aspects of portfolios, things that can't necessarily be assigned a grade or measured according to a set of standards, are important elements in assessing their value. As part of her portfolio research, Sue Ellen Gold of Irvine High School in California asked students to answer the following questions:

— What was the best thing about keeping a portfolio?
— What were the drawbacks?
— Did your writing or thinking change over the semester because you kept a portfolio?
— What was your attitude towards doing your writing? Did this change? Why?

The students mentioned various benefits of keeping portfolios, ranging from the opportunity to monitor their own progress to the chance to "think like writers." Susan, for example, said, "I gained confidence, which is pretty silly, because all I really did was get a folder and put stuff in it. It's funny how a simple folder labeled 'Writer's Portfolio' can give someone confidence in their writing and make her proud to be a writer." Aaron said he became more enthusiastic about writing. "I'm not sure why. I think it is because it was no longer as if I was being forced by some police officer with a grade book point at my head."

Teachers might use this kind of assessment several times during the year, asking students to examine the process for both its benefits and challenges. After all, students do not automatically place a high value on the projects their teachers impose on them (no news to teachers!). By reflecting on portfolios and their effects, students become aware that portfolios can change attitudes and approaches to writing.

Students, as the raison d'etre of the assessment process, can be present at every turn. Maryland's Jim Newkirk, after questioning why he devoted hours of solo time to tabulating percentage grades, brings his middle school students in on the ranking process itself. First, students order each piece they've written during the marking period, from most effective to least. Then they select the best three for an end-of-term assessment conference with Newkirk.

Each conference begins with a discussion of the best pieces, problems they posed and why they surfaced as best. In addition, Newkirk asks students questions like the following:

— Did you complete all the writing goals you set for yourself at the beginning of the term?
— How well did you accomplish them?
— What are your goals for next term?

The three specific goals, which Newkirk approves before each term, become the basis for the students' grades. Portfolios demonstrate how well students have met their goals. Newkirk, a self-described "well-meaning but autocratic instructional leader" turned "facilitator in a student-driven classroom," notes that writing is no longer "stashed and hidden" in folders. It is now visible in portfolios that he uses to help the students become partners in learning.

We also note that linking portfolios in this way to goals set by the students themselves allows them a direct say in both the purpose and assessment of selections. It invites students to take stock of themselves as writers, directing and demonstrating their progress towards goals such as those developed by students in Newkirk's classes: using specific details to support general statements, eliminating unnecessary words, using more sensory details, varying the style and structure of sentences and so on. This tether between portfolios and goals makes progress, which is often elusive, tangible for students.

Interviewing Students about Portfolios

Student-teacher conferences or interviews should occur regularly, at least twice a semester says Arts PROPEL's Dennie Palmer Wolf. Interviews that focus on the students' portfolios and on one or two issues invite students to "pause and look back retrospectively over their portfolios." The kinds of issues Wolf finds most useful to students are:

— Evaluating the differences between a satisfying and less satisfying piece of work ("Why are you happier with one than the other?").

— Finding evidence of progress ("Order the pieces chronologically and discuss the changes and what you think these show that you have learned or discovered about making art. Sometimes you may feel that you have gone backwards instead of forward. If you have a series of works that seem to get 'worse' — that is, the later ones are not as clear, strong or technically proficient as earlier ones — can you order them chronologically and describe what you were thinking or trying to do and ask why it does not seem to be working?").

— Finding evidence of decision-making and/or thinking processes in successive drafts of a selected piece ("Place these in the order in which they were produced and discuss the thinking process that lay behind the successive changes or additions.").

— Finding evidence of an artist or writer in selected pieces that students have chosen as representative of themselves ("What would an outsider, looking at these pieces for the first time, say about the kinds of problems you are dealing with, the kinds of things you are trying to express, the effects you are trying to achieve?").

Wolf suggests asking students to respond to these and similar questions, in writing, before the conferences are held.

Interviews mean something entirely different to Bob Ingalls and other members of the Mt. Vernon High School English department. Here are the questions they ask, as well as examples of responses from the 30 targeted eleventh-grade students who came together and brought their cumulative writing portfolios (three years' worth of selections) to the interview:

— What did your portfolios show you about yourself as a writer? "I feel confident...because when I let other people give me responses they tell me my mistakes then I rewrite it again and then it's a real good writing to me."
— What does your portfolio show that you need to do as a writer? "I don't have much variety. I should experiment with it and try different style of writing."
— Is there anything about your writing that teachers should know? "When I write to a friend and I know it's not being graded, I express myself more but when I know it'll being graded, I don't experiment."

Students begin by writing their responses to the questions (after being fortified with food). Then they move into small- and large-group sessions where teachers listen, tape record their comments, and steer them toward answering larger questions: What does this tell us about the writing you've done as a group in this school? and Is there anything that needs to be done to support you as a writer?

Ingalls and his colleagues offer an exemplary model for teachers who want to extend what portfolios can tell them about teaching and curriculum. Rather than limiting their conclusions about writing at Mt. Vernon to what they alone glean from the portfolios, these teachers have invited students to participate in the process of improving the writing program. They also ask students to reflect on their own reflections; that is, once written, the reflections become part of an exchange, a collective coming to conclusions about what student writers need.

Evaluation: Issues and Concerns

IS IT REALLY NECESSARY TO EVALUATE PORTFOLIOS?

A portfolio is more than a container. Simply collecting writing into a portfolio keeps desks clean, but it serves no particular teaching, learning or evaluation purpose. To call a portfolio a portfolio means doing something more. Nobody said, however, that teachers must use marks to evaluate portfolios. Indeed, many of the teachers we mention in this chapter have abandoned symbols — grades and scores — in favor of new ways to evaluate. They describe, analyze, moderate, discuss, annotate and interview. They think in terms of what they want their students to learn. To paraphrase sociologist William Bruce Cameron, they don't try to count everything that could be counted.

Portfolios are obviously more than the sum of their products or the total of their scores. They are, as Ken Seidman of Jefferson High School notes, a means to an end. When teachers make portfolios primarily a tool for teaching and learning, they do not get carried away with the final judgment day.

HOW DO TEACHERS CHOOSE AN EVALUATION METHOD?

The choices involved in evaluating portfolios may seem staggering. We have deliberately avoided emphasizing one method more than another, believing that the answer does not lie in choosing a particular scoring guide or single letter format. We view evaluation as a rigorous and often experimental procedure that begins with the students as they go through the process of selecting, revising and reflecting. It is a procedure that is linked to the purposes of a particular portfolio project, rather than one drawn from the archives of assessment techniques. Teachers can certainly benefit from understanding the principles of sound assessment, but they must ultimately decide on an evaluation process that is compatible with their own — and the students' — purposes.

DO TEACHERS GRADE PORTFOLIOS?

To grade or not to grade? That is the question many teachers have about portfolios. Once again, purpose is the key. Suppose, for example, teachers decided to use the portfolios to motivate their students as writers. They might choose, as did the Mt. Diablo teachers, to leave the portfolios out of the grading loop. Instead, these teachers made the portfolios the "culminating activity" in their courses, a designation that proved to be more positive for the students than the traditional grade. In contrast, other teachers might argue that students respond most readily to a letter of the alphabet and that to omit grades limits the motivational power of portfolios. Certainly, when grades are called for, the portfolio, with all its demonstrations of long-term effort and process, provides a substantial basis for arriving at a mark. And, if teachers hold off on assigning grades until the time comes to evaluate the portfolio as a whole, they can put the great paper chase behind them. Grading every scrap, after all, is a waste of a teacher's talent.

IN WHAT CASES MIGHT EVALUATION BE UNFAIR?

The subject of assigning grades or scores to portfolios raises the issue of equity. If the stakes are high — that is, if the assigned grade will have serious consequences for individual students — then each must have an equal opportunity to prepare a portfolio of merit. Suppose, for example, that a high school faculty decides to use portfolio assessment to decide the placement of students. Some students have the kind of writing experiences and instruction that allow them to develop a complete portfolio, one filled with a variety of carefully revised pieces. These students are likely to qualify for higher order classes, the kind that help them produce better and better portfolios. Other students may have had fewer opportunities to prepare. As a result, their portfolios are likely to be limp and lean. Denied fair access to adequate preparation, these students go on to situations that too often prevent them from ever producing a proficient writing portfolio. The message here is obvious: ensuring a fair chance for everyone requires good instruction, high expectations, and multiple writing opportunities for all students.

DO PORTFOLIOS HAVE A LIFE

BEYOND THE CLASSROOM?

Getting to know students helps me to like them better and like their writing better.

Peter Elbow

Ron Cabiltes, our high school portfolio hero, prepared his portfolio for two particular audiences. First, he had his classmates in mind as readers. Several of them helped him make his selections and kept him revising. Then, at the end of the marking periods, Ron and other students exchanged portfolios and responded in letters to each other. Ron's second audience was an English teacher at his school, someone other than his own tried-and-true teacher.

This outside-the-classroom audience motivated Ron to put extra effort into his portfolio. It also encouraged him to introduce, document or explain his work carefully, rather than assuming, as students often do, that readers share the identical world. At the same time, Ron was not overloaded with too many audiences or with conflicting audiences. Had he prepared a portfolio for his parents, teachers, friends, counselors, college admission officers, prospective employers and the Wizard of Oz all at once, he would have lost the focus for his selections.

The audience for a portfolio is inextricably tied to the purpose. A single portfolio cannot do everything or be everything to everyone. Ron's selections for a job portfolio would be quite different from those he might make for a demanding English teacher. And, of course, when Ron can pinpoint his audience, he has the power to craft the writing itself for particular readers.

The school community is a ready audience. At Jefferson High School, teacher volunteers throughout the school read 10 portfolios apiece and respond with a letter. Teachers teach each other how to respond effectively. They also teach their students, each of whom responds to a student portfolio from another class. This method places high value on school-wide participation and ensures that every student will have a new audience, both teacher and student, for the portfolio.

The larger community can also become the audience for portfolios. At Central Park East Secondary School in New York City, students present their portfolios to a group of four or five people, including the student's advisor, a staff member, another student and a person of the student's choice. Typically, the student selects a parent, according to teacher Pat Walter, but sometimes the choice is a member of the community. Students present, defend and answer questions about their portfolios as part of their graduation requirement. Members of the audience and the students talk directly to each other and these conversations, in turn, encourage students to reflect on their own writing.

Letting Others Know: How Can Results Be Reported?

When the year ended, Ron's teacher took his portfolio, along with several others, to the school board. They made a big splash. School board members, after all, were used to looking at learning in terms of test scores. Now they could see the learning itself. One member reminisced about the writing he'd done during his own school days, neatly stored in a folder at home. He liked the idea that students made something of their writing. He especially liked hearing what students and teachers had learned from the portfolios; for example, teaching practices that made for exceptional portfolios or student successes with different kinds of writing.

Portfolios call for new ways to present results. The one-number-stands-for-all method of reporting student learning hardly suits the complexities of portfolios. Ron's teachers created a face-to-face situation with school board members in order to make generalizations about what their students were learning and to illustrate those generalizations with the portfolios.

Another group of teachers presented portfolios to their board by having students read selections. This method dramatized the learning and the performance aspect of portfolios. And still another group published a book of selected portfolios for a general audience. In this case, the selections served as exemplars, demonstrating the highest possible student achievement in writing and in reflecting on writing.

In the Vermont portfolio assessment, schools announce the assessment results on school report day. Parents and other community members come to the school to take part in the conversation about the school's writing program and to look at portfolios. The entire community, then, celebrates what is working and discusses what still needs to be done.

Why Make Portfolios Public?

At the heart of all of these reporting innovations are teachers' and students' efforts to make the portfolios mean something to someone else. Why are they going to this trouble? Is there a reason for taking portfolios out of their snug classroom homes?

One reason for making portfolios public is to communicate what is going on in the classroom, department or school. What better demonstration than a selection of real artifacts from real lessons? In addition, portfolios can illustrate notions that are typically hard to communicate, like the idea that individual development is a phenomenon that occurs in fits and starts.

Another reason to go public with portfolios is to enlist support — from administrators, parents, school board members, business leaders and other teachers. By presenting portfolios to their school board, for example, teachers at Jefferson High School were able to secure additional funds for their portfolio program. Another group of teachers, when they passed around portfolios at their faculty meeting, enticed 27 more colleagues to participate in their portfolio efforts. In the same vein, making portfolios available in staff development sessions has encouraged teachers to experiment with portfolios.

Making portfolios public means, of course, that what teachers and students do in their classrooms — the good and the not-so-good — also becomes public. And while we could argue that the public, whoever that might be, will appreciate the inconsistencies and anomalies involved in learning, we also recognize that some audiences will not. It may be important, when portfolios make appearances beyond classrooms and schools, to accompany them with a commentary.

A Movable Feast: Can Portfolios Be Flexible?

Teachers can certainly revise or refine their portfolio design from year to year. In their second year of portfolio assessment, Mt. Diablo teachers, for example, placed greater emphasis on revision, both in the contents of the portfolio and in their classroom teaching because of the sorry state of revision in earlier portfolios. Changing portfolio requirements can also come about because students have grown beyond the original scheme and need more challenges. In contrast to assessments that relentlessly examine the same items in the same format time after time, portfolios give teachers and students permission to tailor the assessment to fit evolving conditions. Because teachers and students can make adaptations, learning as they go along, they can be experimental without fear that an experiment-gone-astray will become another educational millstone.

On the other hand, if teachers want stability from year to year, portfolios can also provide this. For example, teachers at Mt. Diablo High School have, with one exception, varied the contents of the portfolios each year. The single constant is the requirement that students select a piece that demonstrates their ability to state and support an opinion. Because opinion writing has proven, in its portfolio appearances, to be the most challenging kind of writing for students, these teachers want to keep it in the forefront. Similarly, teachers whose purpose is to track development may want to repeat certain features of the design, the presence of particular processes or products. By asking for evidence of revision each year, for example, teachers can compare a student's strategies and results over time.

The Not-Quite-the-Last Word

We hope that no one will ever have the last word on portfolios. The promise of portfolios lies in all their potential variations, in the willingness of the educational community to let them adapt to and serve a range of teaching and learning situations. Too, their value depends precisely on the efforts of teachers and students to examine and reflect on their own work and to make the portfolio representative. Simply putting papers in folders won't do. Nor will letting publishers, testmakers or any other well-meaning outside-the-classroom authorities make the decisions for those who are in the classroom. We recommend avoiding the fancy packaging of commercially published portfolio programs: shrink wrap, colored and pocketed folders, lifetime guaranteed storage boxes, videotaped step-by-step instructions, high-gloss notebooks and cast-in-stone programs. Avoid the last word.

As for this work on portfolios, our last words are about what we have learned so far in our portfolio expedition.

PORTFOLIO ASSESSMENT IS NOT GENERIC

Portfolio assessment is not a brand-name or a one-size-fits-all product. When someone says, "I do portfolios," the logical response is Shakespeare's old question, "What's in a name?" or maybe, "What's in a portfolio?" The word "portfolio," by itself, means little. It's the individual decisions that define the portfolio assessment.

PORTFOLIOS ARE NOT A PANACEA

They will not magically bring whole faculties into harmony or classrooms of students to attention. Even as an assessment tool, they cannot do everything. They are, after all, simply selections made from a whole range of teaching and learning situations. Yet their entrance onto the educational stage has attracted enormous attention, perhaps too much. If teachers and administrators seize upon portfolios, treating them as the newest, most fashionable cure-all, then portfolios may be short-lived or, at the very least, vulnerable to the wear-and-tear of riding the bandwagon.

Imagine a district mandate requiring all teachers to use portfolios, all portfolios to contain identical entries and all entries to emerge from identical classroom conditions. The curriculum, rather than being a rich array of possibilities for students and teachers, would become narrow and standardized, much like the description in our opening poem: "Let ninety thousand reach page 10 by Tuesday." The need for thoughtful teaching would disappear. The opportunity for students to choose and revise and present their work would evaporate in a cloud of constraints. Portfolios would become folders of five or 10 one-shot assessments. Horrified, the entire educational community would begin to long for multiple-choice tests, for any kind of test that interferes less with teaching and learning.

Of course, we place our confidence in exemplary teachers and administrators to resist this kind of automaton approach to portfolio assessment. This book is a testimony to their good sense and imagination in tailoring portfolios to specific needs. They demonstrate what happens when those who teach and learn are responsible for what they do. There will be no portfolio angst as long as portfolios are an extension of the profession's best classroom practices.

PORTFOLIOS MEAN TRADE-OFFS

When in the hands of a single teacher, portfolios are at their most flexible and most accommodating to individual purposes and designs. The minute they become part of a joint venture, let's say one between two neighboring teachers or a group of teachers, their character starts to change. As they begin to make decisions in common, they will likely find themselves making the kinds of compromises they were able to avoid in the isolation of their own classrooms. The trade-off, of course, is that the teachers receive the benefit of conversation, of pooling ideas and resources and perspectives.

If portfolios become part of an even larger operation — for example, a district program — they might lose even more flexibility as more compromises become necessary. Again there is a trade-off — more teachers to talk to in exchange for more uniformity. One situation is not inherently better than another. Rather, each has advantages and disadvantages.

Writing partners work towards a second draft.

PORTFOLIOS NEED NURTURING CLASSROOMS

Portfolios do the most good when they're an integral part of the regular classroom operation. Portfolio users sometimes refer to the portfolio "climate" or "culture" or "spirit," indicating a setting in which youngsters are encouraged and invited to create, revise and reflect continuously. In this setting, portfolios are a vehicle for sustained practice, for frequent self-assessment and for developing useful processes. If portfolios are relegated to being an end-of-year, once-only event, they lose much of their value.

PORTFOLIOS ARE NOT LOGISTICAL MONSTERS

Portfolios do not have to be shipped via freight cars or moving vans to central locations to languish in warehouses. Nor does a school need to convert the baseball field into a holding tank for portfolios. Portfolios belong in classrooms where they'll do some good. Teachers tell us that grocery boxes make ideal storage bins for both writing folders and portfolios (separate boxes for each, of course). File cabinets do just as well, for those who have them. When portfolios need to make some kind of annual trek from one classroom to the next, student assistants are the best moving people we know.

We've talked to teachers who wisely question how much more work portfolios will create. It has occurred to us that readers of this book might be called on to respond to just such a question from their own colleagues. What might they say? How might they suggest that portfolios exchange one kind of work for another? We put together this set of responses (suitable for phone conversations, faculty meeting monologues or reprints in the daily bulletin) to address the inevitable "Why should I?"

— Because you've ruined your social life for too long by marking individual papers and you have this nagging feeling that your efforts are a waste of time.

— Because you're tired of taking on all the responsibility for evaluating your students' work and you've decided it's time to throw the ball into the students' court.

— Because you think a collection of writing, selected and revised, better represents a student as author than any single paper.

— Because marking a stack of similar assignments doesn't tell you everything you want to know (while it may tell you some things you don't want to know).

— Because you and the students will feel a greater sense of accomplishment if you adopt a developmental point of view.

— Because the processes students use — and what they say about these processes — are worth looking at in themselves.

— Because you suspect that learning is more than it appears to be in your fifth — or fourth, or third — period class and that portfolios, with their emphasis on what and how students have learned, might uncover what often gets lost in the relentlessness of class periods.

— Because your teaching and curriculum deserve more than a passing glance — by you and others.

— Because you've always known that assessment legitimately belongs to you and the students and that it must support teaching and learning to be of any value.

— Because it's time, finally, to move beyond the confines of a single assignment, with its finite picture of performance, to a dynamic view of writing and learning to write.

PORTFOLIOS NEED PIONEERS

Portfolios are not new, but writing portfolio assessment in classrooms and schools is a relatively recent phenomenon. We've talked about avoiding the bandwagon syndrome, but we've not said much about the pioneer spirit. When teachers experiment with portfolios, they join a small, but growing, group of explorers. They do a great service to the profession when they share their experiments. This book reflects the generosity of teacher pioneers who willingly contributed to the knowledge of all teachers.

BIBLIOGRAPHY

References

Anson, C. (Ed.) *Writing and Response: Theory, Practice and Research*. Urbana, Illinois: National Council of Teachers of English, 1989.

Askin, W. *Evaluating the Advanced Placement Portfolio in Studio Art*. Princeton, New Jersey: College Entrance Examination Board, 1986.

Atwell, N. *In the Middle: Writing, Reading, and Learning with Adolescents*. New Hampshire: Boynton/Cook, 1987.

Beach, R. "Showing Students How to Assess: Demonstrating Techniques for Response in the Writing Conference." In *Writing and Response: Theory, Practice and Research*. Chris Anson, Ed. Urbana, Illinois: National Council of Teachers of English, 1989.

Cameron, W.B. *Informal Sociology*. New York: Random House, 1963.

Camp, R. *Stimulating Reflection in Arts PROPEL Writing Portfolios*. Princeton, New Jersey: Educational Testing Service, 1989.

Caplan, R. *Writers in Training: A Guide to Developing a Composition Program*. Palo Alto, California: Dale Seymour, 1984.

Daiker, D.A., Sommers, J., Stygall, G., & Black, L. (Eds.) *The Best of Miami's Portfolios*. Oxford, Ohio: Department of English, Miami University, Northwest Regional Educational Library, Portland, Oregon, 1990.

Elbow, P. Keynote Address. New York. National Testing Network in Writing, 1990.

Gold, S.E. "Increasing Student Autonomy through Portfolios." In *In Context: Varieties of Portfolio Practice and Assessment*. K.B. Yancey, Ed. Urbana, Illinois: National Council of Teachers of English (in press).

Healy, M.K. *Using Student Writing Response Groups in the Classroom*. Berkeley, California: Bay Area Writing Project, University of California, Berkeley, 1980.

Herter, R.J. "Writing Portfolios: Alternatives to Testing." In *English Journal*. Vol. 80, no. 1 (1991).

Hilgers, T. "How Children Change as Critical Evaluators of Writing: Four Three-Year Case Studies." In *Research in the Teaching of English*. Vol. 20, no.1 (1986).

Howard, K. "Making the Writing Portfolio Real." In *The Quarterly of the National Writing Project and the Center for the Study of Writing*. Vol. 12, no. 2 (1990).

Kingston, C. Cited by Shirley Bosneil in "Teaching Writing: Problems and Solutions." In *American Association of School Administrators Critical Issues Report*. Sacramento, California: Education News Service, 1982.

Kirby, D. & Kuykendall, C. *Mind Matters: Teaching for Thinking*. Portsmouth, New Hampshire: Heinemann/Boynton/Cook, 1991.

Kirby, D. & Liner, T., with R. Vinz. *Inside out: Developmental Strategies for Teaching Writing*. New Hampshire: Boynton/Cook, 1988.

Krest, M. "Adapting the Portfolio to Meet Student Needs." In *English Journal*. Vol. 76, no. 8 (1990).

Miami University Department of English. *Inviting Students Entering Miami University in 1991 to Participate in the Writing Portfolio Program*. Oxford, Ohio: Miami University, 1991.

Mitchell, R. *Performance Assessment: What It Is and What It Looks Like*. New York: Free Press (in press).

Mohr, M.M. *Revision: The Rhythm of Meaning*. Portsmouth, New Hampshire: Heinemann, 1984.

Murray, D.M. *A Writer Teaches Writing: A Practical Method of Teaching Composition*. Boston, Massachusetts: Houghton Mifflin, 1968.

Myers, M. "The Need for a New Professionalism." In *Teacher as Learner*. M. Chorney, Ed. Calgary, Alberta: Language in the Classroom Project, University of Calgary, 1985.

Newkirk, J. "Portfolio Practice in the Middle School." In *In Context: Varieties of Portfolio Practice and Assessment*. K.B. Yancey, Ed. Urbana, Illinois: National Council of Teachers of English (in press).

Newkirk, T. (Ed.) *Teaching Writing in High School and College*. Portsmouth, New Hampshire: Heinemann, 1990.

Resnick, D. & Resnick, L. Setting a New Standard: Toward an Examination System for the United States. Unpublished proposal. Learning Research and Development Center, University of Pittsburgh, and National Center on Education and the Economy, 1990.

Rief, L. "Finding the Value in Evaluation: Self-Assessment in a Middle School Classroom." In *Educational Leadership*. Vol. 47, no. 6 (1990).

San Diego High School. *Portfolios: A Look at San Diego High's Portfolio Construction and Assessment Process*. Pamphlet, 1990. San Diego High School, 1405 Park Blvd., San Diego, California 92101.

Scott, F.R. *Selected Poems*. Toronto, Ontario: Oxford University Press, 1966.

Thompson, E.H. "Self-Assessment and the Mastery of Writing." In *Testing in the English Language Arts: Uses and Abuses*. J. Beard and S. McNabb, Eds. Rochester, Michigan: Michigan Council of Teachers of English, 1985.

Vermont State Department of Education. *Vermont Writing Assessment: The Pilot Year*. Vermont State Department of Education, 1990.

Wolf, D.P. Developing a "Portfolio Culture" in the Artroom under Various Classroom Conditions. Handout at the California Art Education Association Conference, Sacramento, California, 1990.

Selected Bibliography

Anson, C., Bridwell-Bowles, L. & Brown, R.L. Jr. "Portfolio Assessment across the Curriculum: Early Conflicts." Three papers presented at the National Testing Network in Writing, Minneapolis, Minnesota. Summarized in *Notes from the National Testing Network in Writing, 8*. New York: Instructional Resource Center, City University of New York, 1988.

Askin, W. *Evaluating the Advanced Placement Portfolio in Studio Art*. Princeton, New Jersey: College Entrance Examination Board, 1986.

Au, K., Scheu, J., Kawakami, A. & Herman, P. "Assessment and Accountability in a Whole Language Curriculum." In *The Reading Teacher*. Vol. 43, no. 8 (1990).

Beach, R. "Showing Students How to Assess: Demonstrating Techniques for Response in the Writing Conference." In *Writing and Response: Theory, Practice and Research*. Chris Anson, Ed. Urbana, Illinois: National Council of Teachers of English, 1989.

Beaven, M.H. "Individualized Goal Setting, Self-Evaluation, and Peer Evaluation." In *Evaluating Writing*. C.R. Cooper & L. Odell, Eds. Urbana, Illinois: National Council of Teachers of English, 1977.

Belanoff, P. & Dickson, M. *Portfolio Grading: Process and Product*. Portsmouth, New Hampshire: Heinemann/Boynton/Cook, 1991.

Bingham, A. "Using Writing Folders to Document Student Progress." In *Understanding Writing: Ways of Observing, Learning, and Teaching* (2nd ed.) T. Newkirk and N. Atwell, Eds. Portsmouth, New Hampshire: Heinemann, 1988.

Brandt, R. "On Assessment in the Arts: A Conversation with Howard Gardner." In *Educational Leadership*. Vol. 45, no. 4 (1987).

Burnham, C. "Portfolio Evaluation: Room to Breathe and Grow." In *Training the Teacher of College Composition*. Charles Bridges, Ed. Urbana, Illinois: National Council of Teachers of English, 1986.

Burnett, D. "Giving Credit Where Credit Is Due: Evaluating Experiential Learning in the Liberal Arts." In *Innovative Higher Education*. Vol. 10, no. 1 (1985).

Cambourne, B. & J. Turbill. "Assessment in Whole-Language Classrooms: Theory into Practice." In *The Elementary School Journal*. Vol. 90, no. 3 (1990).

Camp, R. "Changing the Model for the Direct Assessment of Writing." In *Holistic Scoring: New Theoretical Foundations and Validation Research*. M. Williamson & B. Huot, Eds. Norwood, New Jersey: Ablex (in press).

Camp, R. "Thinking Together about Portfolios." In *The Quarterly*. Vol. 12, no. 2 (1990).

Camp, R. & Levine, D. "Portfolios Evolving: Background and Variations in Sixth- through Twelfth-Grade Classrooms." In *Portfolio Grading: Process and Production*. P. Belanoff & M. Dickson, Eds. Portsmouth, New Hampshire: Boynton/Cook, 1991.

Daiker, D.A., Sommers, J., Stygall, G. & Black, L. (Eds.) *The Best of Miami's Portfolios*. Oxford, Ohio: Department of English, Miami University, 1990.

Educational Testing Service. "The Student Writer: An Endangered Species?" In *Focus*. Vol. 23. Princeton, New Jersey: Educational Testing Service, 1989.

Elbow, P. & Belanoff, P. "State University of New York, Stony Brook Portfolio-Based Evaluation Program." In *New Methods in College Writing Programs: Theories in Practice.* P. Connolly & T. Vilardi, Eds. New York: MLA, 1986.

Elbow, P. & Belanoff, P. "Portfolios as a Substitute for Proficiency Examinations." In *College Composition and Communication.* Vol. 37, no. 3 (1986).

Flood, J. & Lapp, D. "Reporting Reading Progress: A Comparison Portfolio for Parents." In *The Reading Teacher.* Vol. 42, no. 7 (1989).

Fowles, M. & Gentile, C. *The Fourth Report on the New York City Junior High School Writing and Learning Project: Evaluation of the Students' Writing and Learning Portfolios (March 1989-June 1989).* Princeton, New Jersey: Educational Testing Service, 1989.

Galleher, D. "Assessment in Context: Toward a National Writing Project Model." In *The Quarterly.* Vol. 9, no. 3 (1987).

Herter, R.J. "Writing Portfolios: Alternatives to Testing." In *English Journal.* Vol. 80, no. 1 (1991).

Hilgers, T. "How Children Change as Critical Evaluators of Writing: Four Three-Year Case Studies." In *Research in the Teaching of English.* Vol. 20, no.1 (1986).

Howard, K. "Making the Writing Portfolio Real." In *The Quarterly.* Vol. 12, no. 2 (1990).

Jongsma, K. "Questions and Answers: Portfolio Assessment." In *The Reading Teacher.* Vol. 43, no. 3 (1989).

Lucas, C. "Toward Ecological Evaluation: Part One." In *The Quarterly.* Vol. 10, no. 1 (1988).

Lucas, C. "Toward Ecological Evaluation: Part Two." In *The Quarterly.* Vol. 10, no. 2 (1988).

Mathews, J.K. "From Computer Management to Portfolio Assessment." In *The Reading Teacher.* Vol. 43, no. 6 (1990).

Meyer, C., Schuman, S. & Angello, N. *NWEA White Paper on Aggregating Portfolio Data.* Lake Oswego, Oregon: Northwest Evaluation Association, 1990.

Mitchell, R. *Performance Assessment: What It Is and What It Looks Like.* New York: Free Press (in press).

Murphy, S. & Smith, M. "Talking about Portfolios." In *The Quarterly.* Vol. 12, no. 2 (1990).

Paulson, L., Paulson, P. & Meyer, C. What Makes a Portfolio a Portfolio? Pre-publication draft, 1990. Available from Northwest Regional Educational Laboratory, Portland, Oregon.

Paulson, F.L. & Paulson, P. How Do Portfolios Measure Up? Paper presented at the Northwest Evaluation Association Conference on Aggregating Portfolio Data, Union, Washington, 1990. Available from Northwest Regional Educational Laboratory, Portland, Oregon.

Pearson, P.D. & Valencia, S. "Assessment, Accountability and Professional Prerogative." In *Research in Literacy: Merging Perspectives. Thirty-Sixth Yearbook of the National Reading Conference.* Rochester, New York: National Reading Conference, 1987.

Rief, L. "Finding the Value in Evaluation: Self-Assessment in a Middle School Classroom." In *Educational Leadership.* Vol. 47, no. 6 (1990).

San Diego High School. *Portfolios: A Look at San Diego High's Portfolio Construction and Assessment Process.* Pamphlet, 1990. San Diego High School, 1405 Park Blvd., San Diego, California, 92101.

Seidel, S. "Even before Portfolios . . . the Activities and Atmosphere of a Portfolio Classroom." In *Portfolio.* Vol. 1, no. 5 (1989).

Simmons, J. "Portfolios as Large-Scale Assessment." In *Language Arts.* Vol. 67, no. 3 (1990).

Spandel, V. & Stiggins, R. *Creating Writers: Linking Assessment and Writing Instruction.* New York: Longman, 1990.

Thompson, E.H. "Self-Assessment and the Mastery of Writing." In *Testing in the English Language Arts: Uses and Abuses.* J. Beard & S. McNabb, Eds. Rochester, Michigan: Michigan Council of Teachers of English, 1985.

Tierney, R., Carter, M. & Desai, L. *Portfolio Assessment in the Reading-Writing Classroom.* Norwood, Massachusetts: Christopher-Gordon, 1991.

Valencia, S. "A Portfolio Approach to Classroom Reading Assessment: The Whys, Whats, and Hows." In *The Reading Teacher.* Vol. 43, no. 4 (1990).

Valencia, S. & Pearson, P.D. "Reading Assessment: Time for a Change." In *The Reading Teacher.* Vol. 40, no. 8 (1987).

Valencia, S. & Pearson, P.D. "Principles for Classroom Comprehension Assessment." In *Remedial and Special Education.* Vol. 9, no. 1 (1988).

Valencia, S., McGinley, W. & Pearson, P.D. "Assessing Reading and Writing." In *Reading in the Middle School.* G. Duffy, Ed. Newark, Delaware: International Reading Association, 1990.

Whittier, S.A. "Portfolio Reflections: Personalizing Education with Portfolios." In *Portfolio*. Vol. 1, no. 4 (1989).

Wiggins, G. "A True Test: Toward More Authentic and Equitable Assessment." In *Phi Delta Kappan*. Vol. 70, no. 9 (1989).

Wolf, D.P. "Opening Up Assessment." In *Educational Leadership*. Vol. 45, no. 4 (1987).

Wolf, D.P., Bixby, J., Glenn, J., Davidson, L. & Gardner, H. "To Use Their Minds Well: Investigating New Forms of Student Assessment." In *Review of Research in Education*. Vol. 17. Washington, D.C.: American Educational Research Association, 1991.

Yancey, K.B. (Ed.) *In Context: Varieties of Portfolio Practice and Assessment*. Urbana, Illinois: National Council of Teachers of English (in press).

Authors' Note

We are deeply grateful to these portfolio pioneers who contributed to the spirit and substance of this book.

ALASKA

Don Cecil, School of Education
University of Alaska, Juneau

CALIFORNIA

Pam Benedetti, Elk Grove High School
Elk Grove Unified School District

Sofia Close, De Anza High School
Richmond Unified School District

Christine Evans, Bernardo Middle School
Poway Unified School District

Mark Hanson, El Capitan High School
Lakeside School District

Darlene Johnson, College View Elementary School
Ocean View School District

Martha Johnson, Academic Skills Center
San Diego State University

Katy Kane
San Diego County Office of Education

Will Lindwall
San Diego City Schools

Mary Ellen Mays, Thousand Oaks High School
Conejo Valley Unified School District

Penny Patton, San Diego High School Writing Academy

Carol Richman, Cuyamaca Model Education Center
Cajon Valley Union School District

Barbara Storms, Youth Opportunities Unlimited
San Diego City Schools

Penny Turk, Greenfield Junior High
Cajon Valley Union School District

John Winbury, Black Mountain Middle School
Poway Unified School District

Helen Ying, English Language Center
Hayward Unified School District

FLORIDA

Dan Kirby, Department of Instructional Programs
University of Central Florida, Orlando

MISSOURI

Michael Allen, Director of Composition/Writing
Northwest Missouri State University

NEVADA

Sally Hellman, Las Vegas High School
Clark County School District

NEW HAMPSHIRE

Linda Rief, Oyster River Middle School
Oyster River Cooperative School District

Jay Simmons, Oyster River High School
Oyster River Cooperative School District

NEW YORK

Pat Walter, Central Park East Secondary School
District 4

NORTH CAROLINA

Dixie Dellinger, Burn High School
Cleveland County School District

VERMONT

Geof Hewitt, State Department of Education
Montpelier

VIRGINIA

Bob Ingalls, Mt. Vernon High School
Fairfax County